metahuman
destinations

volume one

*Thank you for supporting independent publishing
and the work of the Systemology Society*

mardukite.com

MARDUKITE ACADEMY 2—VOLUME SECOND EDITION

metahuman
destinations

VOLUME ONE:
COMMUNICATION, CONTROL & COMMAND

BY JOSHUA FREE

THE JOSHUA FREE IMPRINT
JFI PUBLICATIONS

Also available in hardcover.

A MARDUKITE SYSTEMOLOGY PUBLICATION
Mardukite Research Library Catalogue No. "Liber-2C"
Developed for Mardukite Academy & Systemology Society
Previously published in one volume as Liber-Two—
"Metahuman Destinations: Piloting the Course to Homo Novus"
cum superiorum privilegio veniaque
TWO-VOLUME SECOND EDITION
August 2023

Published from
Joshua Free Imprint – JFI Publications
Mardukite Borsippa HQ, San Luis Valley, Colorado

The Original Grade-IV Systemology Professional Piloting Course

Take your First Steps beyond the Master Grades toward

Metahuman Destinations

with a *Book* that *launched* the *Wizard Levels*

The landmark public debut of Grade-IV Mardukite Systemology and a foundation stone for reaching higher Level Awareness while taking back command and control of Self as Spirit.

Fundamental keys to elevating *'Actualized Awareness'* and uncovering the latent abilities of *Self* to properly direct a relay of energy and power of *Intention* in the Universe—and thus command *'Control Centers'* of the Human Condition... those experienced as the *'Mind–Body Connection'*.

Discover a redefined future of what it means to be human with the first of a new Mardukite Academy 2-Volume Edition for Metahuman Destinations: Piloting the Course to Homo Novus. This presentation of Volume One includes Unit-1 (Liber-2C) "Communication, Command and Control." In brief...

<u>Communication</u> is an *"energetic flow"* of *Intention* to cause an effect (or *Duplication*) at a distance; it is the personal energy moved (or acted upon by *Will*), or else *"selectively directed attention"*; and it consists primarily of a *"messenger action"* used to transmit and receive a particle (or wave) of energy across a medium, or across *"space."*

A complete esoteric understanding of communication awaits you!

Experience the "2020 Professional Piloting Course" with two-volumes filled with spiritual technology for all Systemologists. Together we can help *Pilot* the destiny of Human Evolution toward ideals that will free the Human Condition and return control of *Life* back to the Spirit.

*Based on the first 'Grade-IV'
Premiere 'Class-2C' Piloting and Processing
Professional Course Lectures given
by Joshua Free to the Systemology Society
Spring 2020 to Autumn 2020*

Also contained in the complete Grade-IV anthology:
The Metahuman Systemology Handbook

METAHUMAN DESTINATIONS
VOLUME-ONE
TABLET OF CONTENTS

This material is continued in:
Volume Two: The Universe and Mind-Body Connection

Titles in <u>The Pathway to Self-Honesty</u> Grade-III Series:

Systemology: The Original Thesis

The Power of Zu

The Tablets of Destiny (Revelation)

Crystal Clear: Handbook for Seekers

"Basics" abridged pocket anthology available as:

The Way Into The Future

A complete Grade-III anthology is also available as:

The Systemology Handbook

Titles in <u>The Gateways of Infinity</u> Grade-IV Series:

Metahuman Destinations

Imaginomicon

The Way of the Wizard

A complete Grade-IV anthology is also available as:

The Metahuman Systemology Handbook

...more amazing volumes coming soon!

∞

EDITOR'S NOTE

"The Self does not actualize Awareness
past a point not understood."
—*Tablets of Destiny*

While preparing this book for publication, the editors
have made every effort to present this material in a
straightforward manner—using clear, easy to read and
understand language.

Wherever a word that is defined in the glossary
first appears in the two volumes, it will be **bold**.

A clear understanding of this material is critical for
achieving actual realizations and personal benefit
from applying philosophies of *Mardukite Zuism* and
NexGen Systemology spiritual technology.

The *Seeker* should be especially certain not to simply
"read through" this book without attaining proper
comprehension as "knowledge." Even when the
information continues to be "interesting"—if at any
point you find yourself feeling lost or confused while
reading, trace your steps back. Return to the point of
misunderstanding and go through it again.

It is expected that a *Seeker* will work through this
material multiple times to achieve optimum results.

And *now* responsibility for this power and its
actualization is passed on to you, the *Seeker*.

Take nothing within this book on faith.
Apply the information directly to your life.

Decide for yourself.

∞

METAHUMAN DESTINATIONS

— ENTRY POINTS —

MARDUKITE SYSTEMOLOGY
GRADE-IV INTRODUCTION

:: An Introduction to the Basic Course ::

"THIS IS SYSTEMOLOGY"
A GRADE-III HISTORY & OVERVIEW
summation presented by David Zibert[*]

Since the **inception** of the **NexGen Systemology** Society nearly a decade ago, many things have been brewing quietly and unseen in the underground; but, fear not, as slowly but surely, everything will be brought to light...as "New Babylon" *is rising.*

The original literary presentation of NexGen Systemology occurred underground in 2011 and continued through 2013. The essential materials from this period were recently reissued as *"Systemology: The Original Thesis"* by Joshua Free. These materials first began to appear in 2011 with a series of booklets by Joshua Free, which at first glance were actually quite different from anything he had really presented before. The booklets were the first to present "Systemology"—or else, work of the "Systemological Society," an offshoot of the Mardukite Research Organization and extension of the Mardukite Chamberlains group that previously participated in the development of the Grade-II Mardukite Core.[∞]

"Systemology" means "system logics"—or else, "the logics behind the systems," which is also to say, in more esoteric terms, "the magic behind the magic."

In 2011, several booklets were released for the "original thesis" Systemology series; the first one titled—*"Human, More Than Human: Awakening to the Next Evolution."* It was really a down to earth approach; a really simple user-friendly booklet about how, quite literally, "Humans are

---

[*] Based on a presentation given to the "Mardukite Chamberlains" and "Systemology Society" by David Zibert in November 2019.

[∞] The Grade-II Esoteric Research Library is collected in its entirety within *"Necronomicon: The Complete Anunnaki Legacy"* (2020 Master Edition Hardcover) by Joshua Free.

more than Human"—that we are more than simply our physical body and that there are really "worlds" out there that most individuals are unaware of in their daily lives. It was really just taking the reader by the hands and saying in a rather basic and gentle way how *we are more than human.*

The original underground release and presentation of Systemology was quite peculiar at the time. Even I wasn't sure what the goal was behind all this. But in the end, it made sense—and there was a brief follow-up published soon after: "*Systemology Defragmentation: Self-Honesty for the Next Evolution.*" This title delved into the core of the matter and explained the basic "defragmentation" process, which is the same as **ascension** up the "Ladder of Light" as we know it from the *Grade-II* presentation and the more commonly known Babylonian paradigm.

Systemology presented the core pathway; the same pathway intended with the previous "Mardukite Core" and our explorations into the Babylonian paradigm proper, but these new booklets presented the main tenets of this core without some of the more esoteric, magical or religious semantic trappings that we commonly find with literal interpretations of the *Arcane Tablets.*

A third booklet comprising the "original thesis" arrived in 2012 as "*Transhuman Generations: The Next Evolution of a Species.*" This one relates how worldviews are programmed in the generational cycles that repeat itself over an over. And, of course, when most individuals are unaware of that taking place, such as we see in the world that we live in, history is bound to repeat itself. Although the material is quite basic, it is really important information for Self-**Actualization.**

Another installment, completing the "original thesis," appeared in 2013, titled "*Systemology For Life: Patterns and Cycles.*" This one continued in the spirit of "*Transhuman Generations,*" but this relayed material about personal cycles—and about cycles repeating themselves—yes, through the generations, but more specifically, cycles repeating themselves as we experience them as individuals: how to notice them, and to go beyond them, of course, toward the goal of *Self-Honesty* which is, again, achieved via **"defragmentation."**

It is these materials—that I've just mentioned—that are gathered together into the small anthology reissued now as *"Systemology: The Original Thesis."*[∞] In addition to these, there were a few other small underground releases that were not as widely circulated. One of these being *"The Games: Portals of Self-Transformation & The Underground Occult Initiation."*[*] This was a very controversial booklet when it was published; it relayed the exploratory adventure of Joshua Free in the West Coast Occult Underground.

It became apparent in 2013 that many individuals, even those among the Mardukite network still studying the *Grade-II* "Mardukite Core," were not ready for Joshua Free's new "Systemology" developments as a whole. Very few outside the small network of the "NexGen Systemological Society" really took notice of what we working toward from 2011 to 2013—and continued to work even more quietly and unnoticed thereafter. Of course, this was all about to change with a reboot that is presently going on now as we enter the 2020's.

One of the very interesting aspects of "Mardukite Systemology" is experienced by one who has been actually following the work of Joshua Free from the beginning—and seeing how "Systemology" *was* the goal; seeing how it was the *goal* all along since the very beginning and the inception of the Mardukite Ministries and the Mardukite Research Organization in 2008. Anyone who has read the introductory material of the *"Necronomicon: The Anunnaki Bible"* or *"The Complete Anunnaki Bible"* by Joshua Free— even those individuals that have read his *Arcanum* book—

∞   Reissued as *"Systemology: The Original Thesis of Mardukite New Thought"*; reprinted in the *"Systemology Handbook."*

*   Portions of the text included in *"Systemology: Original Thesis."*

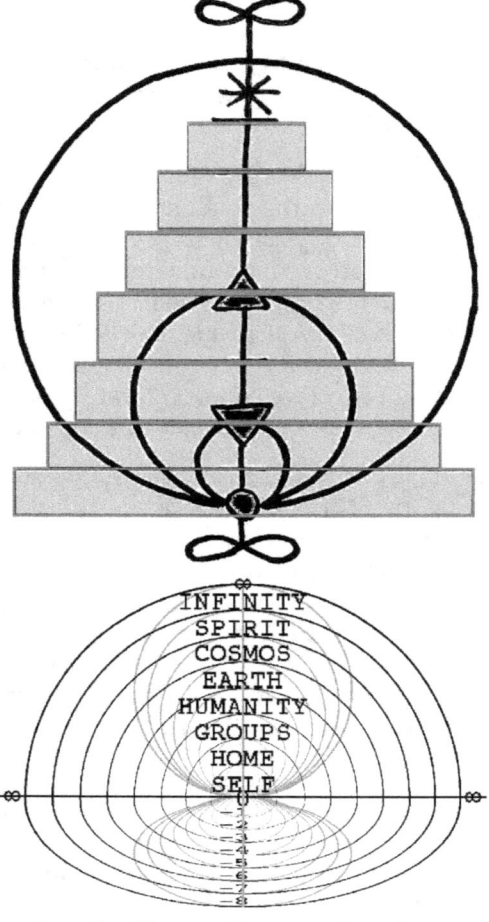

will notice that the "logic of systems" and an aim toward the applied spiritual technology of a "Systemology" is what is underlying the journey and is what has been there all along, driving the work forward.

In October 2019, the NexGen Systemology Society experienced a new public debut with the arrival of its first true core textbook, **catalogued** as *Mardukite Systemology "Liber-One,"* released globally as *"The Tablets of Destiny: Using Anci-*

ent Wisdom to Unlock Human Potential"‡ from the new Joshua Free Publishing Imprint. It concisely presents the fundamental foundation for "Mardukite Systemology" itself—upon which further Systemology discourses are now built upon.

"*The Tablets of Destiny*" (*Liber-One*) is *not* a rehash of what was done before (in "*Systemology: The Original Thesis*")—it is actually a completely new presentation of material. It presents the logics behind the systems, of what the "Mardukite Chamberlains" had discovered concerning Babylon. It's like: "Okay, we found *that*. Now, *what* do we *do* with it? —And how does everyone get *benefit* from it?" Now, this is where we are. This is what we do. So, now what is this "*Grade-III Mardukite Systemology*" you may ask?

At the most basic core: it is an applied spiritual technology of the 21st century AD based on the spiritual wisdom from the 21st century BC, which were compiled in their rawest tablet form in the *Grade-II* Mardukite Core—"*The Complete Anunnaki Bible*," "*Sumerian Legacy*," &tc. Launching *Grade-III, Liber-One* introduces what we have termed the "**Standard Model**" (of Systemology), otherwise known as the "*ZU-Line*" (in Mardukite Zuism). This, in itself, is a workable non-dogmatic and applied model of the same Babili Ladder of Lights—the StarGates of this Universe—of which you should already be familiar with from *Grade-II* work.

So, how does the "Standard Model" or "ZU-Line" work? First of all, these are abstract constructs, graphically defining **parameters** for a Systemology of the Human Condition. It is divided as *seven*—or *eight*—steps for practical purposes, but theoretically extends to Infinity, above and below its scale; just like the Ladder of Lights paradigm of *Gates*, or any such similar Kabbalistic Model.

---

‡ Available in the complete Grade-III "*Systemology Handbook*"; revised as "*The Tablets of Destiny (Revelation): Using Long-Lost Anunnaki Wisdom to Change the Fate of Humanity.*"

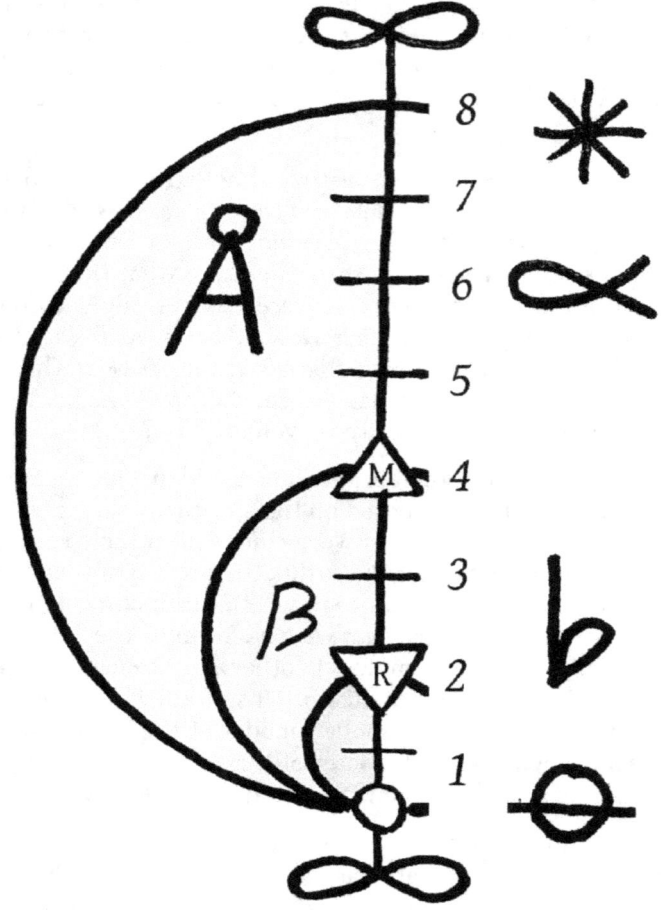

"*The Tablets of Destiny*" (*Liber-One*) focuses on the lower levels of the scale—from *0-to-4*. This work emphasizes building a strong personal foundation of health and strength before the individual is introduced to more advanced practices—such as those included in its follow up manual, "*Crystal Clear*" (*Liber-2B*) and the other upper-level Grades. But, most importantly, we found out that a sane "Mind-Body Connection" is a prerequisite to experiencing a Self-Honest, clear and unfragmented **realization** of Self as "I-AM-**Alpha-Spirit**" in this lifetime.

This new approach is actually quite different from previous attempts in other traditions; even the most pious *Gnostic* paradigms still continue to reject material **existence**—what we refer to as **"beta-existence"**—as an "illusion." We are not rejecting the Physical Universe in Mardukite Systemology; no, rather we are agreeing that such is an artificial ordination of an otherwise very real universe in which the Human being, as a **"genetic vehicle,"** is the tool used to experience of such a reality. Lower **gradients** of the ZU-line (Standard Model) run as follows—but, be aware that these descriptions are something of an over simplification; there is more to it, though this should suffice for our present review:

0 — Inert Matter (theoretical zero, since everything in existence is basically a motion), or else Body Death (for the "genetic vehicle");

1 — Physical Body (basic **physiological** functions/cellular "fight/flight") receiving communications from...

2 — **Reactive Control Center** (or "RCC") which includes survival programming ("reactive response mechanism") inherent to the development and experience of all physical life.

Between "1" and "2" lies the standard emotional range of the Human Condition, which can be, and is, programmed and encoded with *imprints* preventing the Self access to its own experience of higher levels in Self-Honesty.

3 — Thought (**associative-knowledge**) and activity communicated from...

4 — **Master Control Center** (or "MCC") which is the point of contact from the True Self, or Higher Self in some paradigms, and is the highest gradient relating to the genetic vehicle or physical body for the Human Condition in the Physical Universe.

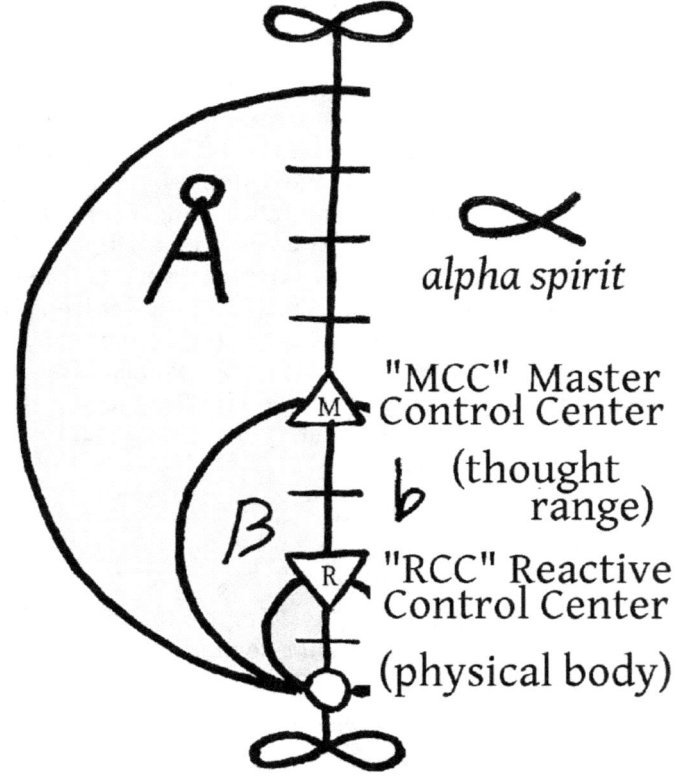

alpha spirit

"MCC" Master Control Center

(thought range)

"RCC" Reactive Control Center

(physical body)

Self-Honesty is to be sought at each of these gradients as one moves upward on the "Pathway." This means that, for example, if you are not at a point of Self-Honesty regarding gradient "1" and "2," then you won't be certain to have a Self-Honest command of the thoughts and programming beyond that, which is preventing you from experiencing the knowing and beingness of your Higher or True Self; which we refer to as the state of the "Alpha Spirit," a spiritual being which merely maintains **considerations** of experiencing a beta-existence. In effect what is sought on this "Pathway" is a clear **communication** with the **continuity** of All Life—and that starts with your own—and when you have a Self-Honest experience of your own life, you practice the same for ALL Life at each

Sphere of Existence, or else you ain't being truly Self-Honest. This systematic process—as we present it in "Systemology"—begins with removal of emotional imprinting; all irrationality is coming from the Reactive Control Center (RCC) and so cannot be properly analyzed by the Master Control Center (MCC). This means that most people live their life in a reactionary fashion, often under the control of their emotions without even knowing it.

Here, it is important to mention, that what is implied by references to "emotions" really concerns the negative states of the Human Condition—which are all reactionary in nature—such as hopelessness, fear, anger, lust, jealousy, and so forth. For example: usually when you are angry, you are operating as a reaction to something—and the encoded mechanisms are commanded by the Reactive Control Center (plotted at "2.0" on the Standard Model or ZU-line). This is quite different from experiences of more positive states, such as being "in love" or personal enthusiasm about **willingness** to act on something, &tc., which puts the individual at *cause*, rather than as the *effect*, and which are commanded by the Master Control Center (4.0).

Much of the Mardukite (NexGen) Systemology paradigm could be summed up as returning the Self to the state of being Cause rather than the Effect. You always should be able, at all times, by using the Master Control System through thought control, take notice when your Reactive Control Center takes over through emotions, and even correct accordingly with Self-Processing.* Eventually, pre-programmed automated reactivity is dissolved altogether —and that's Self-Honesty; *is* our "Systemology" in a nutshell. Again, there is much more to this, but the important part to take away about these "levels" is that Self-Honesty is to be sought at each *gradient*—and the Seeker will quickly discover that these act as *Gateways* to accessing increasingly higher points of Actualized **Awareness.**

---

* See *Liber-2B*, released in 2019 as *"Crystal Clear"* by Joshua Free; also contained in the Grade-III *"Systemology Handbook."*

One basic method to systematically process "emotional imprinting" is described fully in *"The Tablets of Destiny"* (*Liber-One*). There are many other practical processes within *Grade-III* material included in *"Crystal Clear"* (*Liber-2B*).

The basic theory supporting the Standard Model and *ZU-line* is a simple **cosmology** rooted from the lore contained on *Arcane Tablets* from **Mesopotamia**. Simply put: you have **"AN"** which is the *"Spiritual"*; and **"KI"** which is the *"Physical"*; between which exists a **continuum** called **"ZU,"** which manifests as *"Life"* or else *"Spiritual Life Awareness."* A more specific discourse on the nature of "ZU" is the subject of a supplemental [delivered in lecture format by Joshua Free in December 2019 and then released in print form as *"The Power of Zu: Increasing Control of the Radiant Energy in Everyday Life"* with a foreword by Reed Penn.]

Great care has been taken with *"Tablets of Destiny"* (*Liber-One*) so that everything in the book is as clear a message as possible—even for a novice—including a concise definition of each word that could be problematic or misunderstood, and also definitions for the vocabulary introduced newly in our Systemology. Furthermore, *Liber-One* includes a summary of each lesson, given at the end of a chapter for optimal clarity. I also found that these summaries are great for just a quick second reading and review.

Yes, we are aware that some people will see *"Tablets of Destiny"* and *"Crystal Clear"* as just another mere "Self-Help" book series—which from a certain perspective this *is* a "Self-Help" series—but my take on this is that apparent these "Self-Help" books containing "deep esoteric occult wisdom" makes for a great change from all those books posing as "deep esoteric occult wisdom" and yet turn out to be mere Self-Help books that provide "no help."

As it's written: "Don't take anything from these books by faith. Apply these principles directly to your life..." to confirm that these are true for you from the perspective of Self and thus discover, and live, the life you were meant to live, Self-Honestly as a Free Spirit.

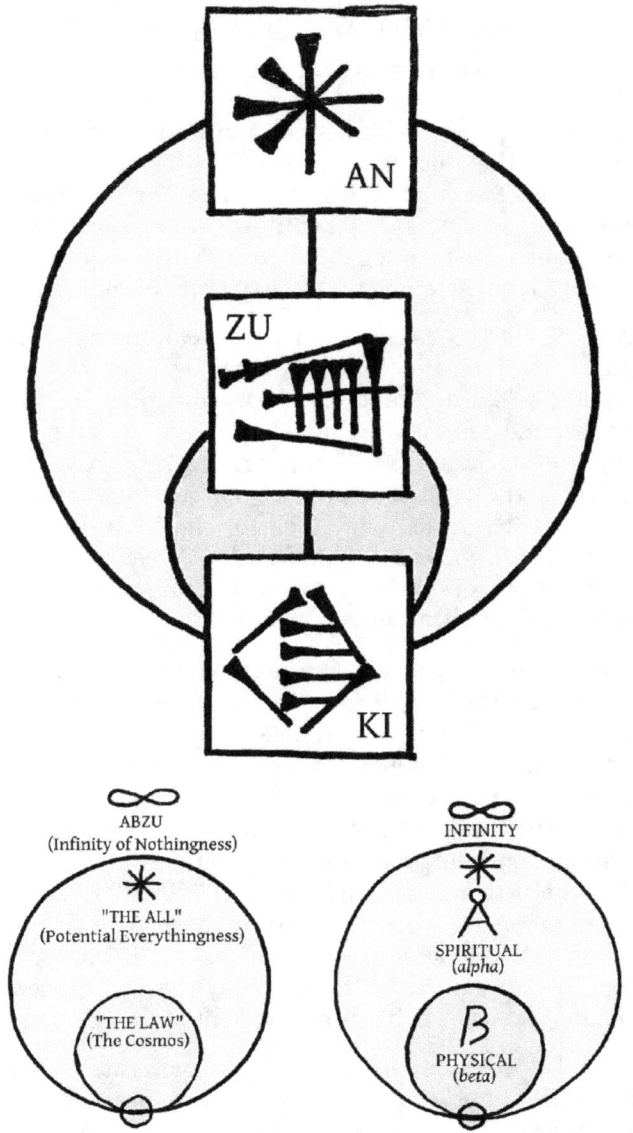

PROFESSIONAL PILOTING PROCEDURES COURSE
GRADE-IV SYSTEMOLOGY INTRODUCTION
based on lectures by Joshua Free

SYSTEMOLOGY is the practical application of "**systems theory**" to the study and spiritual experience of *Life, the Universe and Everything*. This "technology" is referred to as "NexGen Systemology," **Mardukite Systemology** and/or "Metahuman Systemology" in order to distinguish it from other academic sciences and modern uses of the term.

MARDUKITE SYSTEMOLOGY is a developing product or result from intensive work conducted by an official extension of the "Mardukite Research Organization" in 2010, as directed and recorded by mystic philosopher and underground esoteric author, Joshua Free. *Systemology* work is treated as the practical spiritual philosophy and technology accessible to us today (and for the future) from the oldest cuneiform writings and Arcane Tablets set down in ancient **Babylon**—in the heart of **Mesopotamia** and "**Sumerian**" civilization.

There are also those Seekers that will treat this same material (below the knowledge "Grade" of Systemology) in an exclusively religious or mystical appreciation as MARDUKITE ZUISM—although the two are not mutually exclusive. At this time we are treating *NexGen Systemology* as the "upper level" applied spiritual philosophy, techniques for spiritual counseling and spiritual evolution (Self-Actualization) methodology *of* the former "religious" understanding of *Mardukite Zuism*, in any of its derivative forms, including "Mesopotamian Neopaganism" or "Hermetic Mysticism" or any surviving faction today that has tapped the 'stream' that leads behind the "Ancient Mystery School."

"Grade-IV Metahuman Systemology" materials delivered within this "intermediate course" are presented in a straightforward and direct manner so that they may be understood by anyone—to the extent or level an individual has actualized a "ledge" of understanding for. For this reason our previous Grades of Research and Discovery, which a Seeker may study, are structured to represent three "levels" of understanding leading toward a basic state of "**Self-Honesty**."

The subject of each Grade is always the same: *Life, the Universe and Everything.* The only factor that differs is the "**level**" of understanding used to treat the study and practice of information. *"Cultural"* and *"language"* themes are another factor that tends to differ across the historical timeline on Earth. We resolve many of these semantic issues in "Grade III" when working toward a standard universally applicable terminology, demonstrable as the "**Standard Model** of Systemology"—which includes the "*ZU-line.*" The premise behind current work is provided in *"Grade-III Mardukite Systemology"* material available in core *Grade-III* textbooks—*The Tablets of Destiny* and *Crystal Clear* —both of which are collected within the Master Edition *Grade-III* anthology: *The Systemology Handbook.*

Application of Systematic Self-**Processing** developed only after a decade of additional esoteric experimental research privately conducted by remote members of the underground "Systemological Society." This ongoing exploration into "applied spiritual philosophy" is established in light of all collected wisdom from various mystical and spiritual pursuits during the last 6,000 years of record history—most of which is found to be either erroneous and/or unworkable in effectively producing consistent results toward a higher state of Actualized Awareness.

The functional purpose of "Systemology Processing"— whether performed by one's *Self* alone out of a workbook (like *Crystal Clear*), with the assistance of a friend or by a "professional systemology **pilot**"—is for a *Seeker* to effectively <u>actualize</u> true <u>realizations</u> that produce positive movement on what is referred to as THE PATHWAY TO SELF-HONESTY—which is also the technical designation for *Grade-III* materials otherwise referred to as "Mardukite Systemology."

During a twenty-five year engagement with the underground esoteric and "New Age" community, Joshua Free
discovered that the majority of practitioners following the
"Route of Magick and Mysticism"* or "Route of Druidism
and Dragon Legacy"‡ (and other esoteric traditions amal-
gamated from diverse well known "organizations,"
"orders" and "fellowships") were not independently arriv-
ing at the intended *realizations* from these philosophies,
much less an *actualization* of the same.

This is one of the stumbling blocks that Joshua Free discovered concerning most contemporary approaches to
"enlightenment" and metaphysical "Self-Help" regimens.
One primary goal of systemology—which should be evident in the systematic presentation and demonstrable
"Self-Processing" techniques in *Grade III*—is to raise an individual's ("*Seeker's*") state of Actualized Awareness. This
requires, by definition, bringing what is hidden into the
light, or else carrying those aspects of "**consciousness**" that
exist below the level of analytical surface thought up to
such levels where they may be treated "consciously" by
Self—the true and actual *spiritual Self;* what we call the "**Alpha Spirit.**"

Raising a *Seeker's* "level" of *Awareness—Actualized Awareness*—means very simply bringing more of an individual's
"actual present space-time" (beta) *Awareness* in "**phase**"
or "synch" with the "Alpha Spirit" (the True "I-AM" Self).
This brings the power and attention of *Awareness* more under the control of the *Seeker*, which is to say "clear
communications" of *actual* potential.

> "It is my goal for NexGen Systemology that we can
> elevate the *Actualized Awareness* of all *Seekers*—all
> *Humans*—on Earth to provide a true vehicle for
> their spiritual evolution in Self-Honesty. It is the

---

*   Treated as "*Grade-I Part-A*" by *Mardukite Academy*; refer to
     "*The Great Magickal Arcanum*" by Joshua Free.

‡   Treated as "*Grade-I Part-D*" by *Mardukite Academy*; refer to
     "*Merlyn's Complete Book of Druidism*" by Joshua Free.

duty of every Systemology Pilot and Mardukite Minister to bring the conscious *Awareness* of all *Humanity* up and out from the murky muddy heavy sticky **dross** that they are subjected to; all of the solidarity and barriers leading to the acceptance that we must remain confined and entrapped only to the lowest level of conceptual consideration. It is by cumulatively shedding skin and layers of everything that is not the true I-AM Self that a *Seeker* ascends through sequential Gates of Higher Understanding—meaning true realization in 'Self-Honesty' and *Actualized Awareness*."

Grade-IV is clearly an intermediate stepping stone between two great planes of realization:

a.) what has come before—treated as the "Master" levels, including basic *Grades I-II,* and the *Grade-III* "Pathway to Self-Honesty" distinguishing "Mardukite Systemology"; and

b.) what we are now leading into—using *Grade-IV* as a launch point toward higher "Wizard" levels, distinguishing the "Actualized Technician" (A.T.) Grades still forthcoming.

It is easy to differentiate between material from the "**Master Grades**" (*I-III*) and the newer level of experimentation for "Professional Piloting Procedure" at *Grade-IV.* At this present Grade of research and discovery, both the Pilot *and* Seeker are developing skills, earning education and strengthening personal certainty of the "Alpha Spirit" as an "Actualized Technician" of spiritual technology.

Joshua Free first announced the integration of "Systematic Self-Processing" and "Professional Piloting" into Mardukite Systemology during a lecture given on August 9, 2019.[*]

---

[*] Transcripts appear in the premiere edition of *"The Tablets of Destiny"*; reprinted in the *"Systemology Handbook."*

"There are many solitary methods of heightening Awareness and increasing mental skills necessary for 'processes,' but I bring up this example... because when engaged in [professional] processing, there are two people involved: one of them is going through the 'processing' toward Self-Honesty and one of them is assisting from a point of Self-Honesty. We identify the one receiving the service, or going through the 'processing,' as the Seeker. In order to differentiate a very specific role that the assistant has in this process, the individual administering the 'processes' is referred to as the Pilot. And let me make this point clear from the get go: the Pilot is specifically and exclusively responsible for Self-Honestly assisting the Seeker in reaching their chosen *destination*—nothing more or less. The Pilot is not a tour guide; not an interpreter; not a doctor; certainly not a therapist in the traditional sense—they are offering no actual advice toward or against anything that is uncovered as a result of systematic processing. Any and all realizations are meant for the Seeker to discover, determine and actualize on their own. The Seeker merely has the confidence now of knowing there is a safety net of travel by someone who has already been where they want to go!"

Based on this description, your first thoughts may be that this *Grade-IV* course must pertain exclusively to some rigorous "procedures" and esoteric philosophies that are useful only to those upper-level students of our underground brand of dispensed knowledge. This could not be any further from the truth. *Anyone* can benefit from the basic instruction and applied spiritual philosophies explained and demonstrated throughout this book.

Many believe that the purpose of all true spiritual, mystical and philosophical avenues or "routes" engaged as paradigms to treat the experience and interaction of *Life, the Universe and Everything* are headed in the "same direction" and are to be held in equal regard. If truth, the historical timeline and demonstrable workable effectiveness are any definitive indicators, we can be most certain that the resulting "destination" for the plethora of "routes to knowledge" brewed within the intellectual labyrinths of the "human condition" are anything but equal to one another. In fact, what—if anything—could be truly demonstrated as "equal" in its actual properties of existence and interaction in this solidified and condensed "physical universe" (which we call "*beta existence*") unless we are referring to the exact "same" thing in two spots in space?

Such *is* actually possible, though the "**human condition**" tends not to experience such phenomenon at the mundane levels of "**standard issue**" sensory reception. In fact, "**associative knowledge**" and the inability to *distinguish* "things" in the universe is one of the primary sources of "personal **fragmentation**"—which is one of the main subjects of our systemology.

The purpose of systemology and systematic piloting is to support responsibility of the Prime Directive of all *Life, the Universe and Everything*—which is *to exist* and to act toward a continuation of *existence*—and for this purpose: to actualize the highest reach as "cause" on the spheres, which is to say "**defragmenting**" or clearing energetic channels all the way up to our highest states of knowing and being, or otherwise Actualized Awareness.

Being a high-level "cause" means the Self-directed communication and control of energy and power in such a manner as to consistently act toward the continuation of personal existence at is highest and truest "**Alpha**" state. This means Self-directing effects that will promote the highest ideals of "utility" on the Zu-line and its reach across the Spheres of existence from the **point-of-view (POV)** of *Self* here in this moment as it experiences the physical continuity of a low-level densely solidified universe as *beta-existence*.

A systemologist soon learns the fastest route toward actualizing the highest extent of reach as "cause" is to act toward assisting all existence insofar as it mutually helps to maintain the Prime Directive at all levels—"help" being one of the highest forms of communication, which not only allows an individual to *be* at a position of *cause*, but also increases energy frequencies on the Zu-line (which satisfy the necessary requirements of a Prime Directive). The ability to extend our reach as "cause" is accelerated by the "help" and "assistance" of whatever we may take responsibility for, even if its only going to be a responsibility of being in communication with the universe; any universe.

When we consider the role of Pilots in Systemology—they are helping and assisting a Seeker, which in turn is helping and assisting the Pilot's reach on the Prime Directive. A Seeker must be willing *to be* helped and assisted—and be willing to help and assist the Pilot—by providing a full "attention" (presence) for participation in the session and processing communications.

Academic and practical emphasis of the first *Grade IV* installments concerns defragmentation of **communication**, personal communication systems and control of the same (*Liber-2C* and *Liber-2D*). In no short time it will become completely evident just why this is so important; particularly as a stable orientation point to launch higher grades. With that resolved, the second part of *Grade IV* prioritizes instruction and techniques (*Liber-3C* and *Liber-3D*) that put personal power and creative energy of the **imagination** back under full determination of Self.

With tools and training provided as *Grade-IV "Professional Piloting Procedure,"* an interested reader, *Seeker* or *Master* may strongly benefit from attaining greater certainty of control over personal <u>communication</u> and <u>imagination</u> as Self-directed by **Will** and Intention.

"And when one truly realizes the full considerations that a combination of <u>communication</u> and <u>imaginat-</u>

ion truly has upon the individual, an entirely new or previously unreachable universe of possibilities suddenly becomes real again; becomes a potential Reality again within the reach of Self as Alpha Spirit. Each an every one of us is a participant in the creation of universes and realities and we have the responsibility to our Self to permit the highest freedom of the Alpha Spirit to once again unfold as the present Awareness as Self. This is a state that is completely within reach of all individuals on planet Earth today; all we have to do is free ourselves to create a better world. So, let's get together and help one another create a better world."

OBJECTIVES AND GOALS OF GRADE-IV METAHUMAN SYSTEMOLOGY
based on a lecture by Joshua Free*

Completion of the "Core" for *Grade-III Mardukite Systemology* allowed our work to move up to a new level of understanding and practicality; and now we are able to speak from an even greater, higher, more widely encompassing perspective as *Grade-IV Professional Piloting Procedure*. We are still moving upward on the *Pathway* and not simply restricting this knowledge-to what applies exclusively to *Piloted* processing. We are dealing with new vistas for our understanding and are achieving significant advancements toward our true end goals at an accelerated rate. But it is important that we do not miss any steps along the way; and this important for all *Seekers*, whether *Pilots* or otherwise. It is apparent to many that we have tapped into something here that shifts us up and beyond what we find at the *Master Grades*, but it is wholly dependent on true realizations that were in reach up to this point.

Grade-IV builds upon instruction given as the *Grade-III* "Master" level of Mardukite work that precedes our present "Wizard" *Grades*. To make certain no stone has remained unturned, a Seeker is prompted systematically through the *Grade-III* work as an integral of *Grade-IV,* and combined, the "whole package" is intended to yield very specific attainable goals. Before we move a *Seeker* beyond *Grade-IV* there are certain things we expect from processing taking place and realizations held. There is no question that an adequate education of true knowledge can accelerate this journey—but this is only on an assumption that a *Seeker* is ready to receive and interpret the information. Otherwise, its just more data to add to a heap.

We have all made decisions, however much they may be influenced by other-determined sources, about what we

---

* Given to the Systemology Society the evening of 15, May 2020.

are *willing* to be, *willing* to do, *willing* to have a communication with—and *Self* does not like to be wrong. So, here we are now trying to unwrap this mess of convoluted beliefs and agreements we made as Self along the way. You would think it should be an easy task, but the Human Condition is very much tied to the "physical" way of things—and the more greatly an Alpha Spirit identifies *Self* or *"I"* with this "physical" way of things, it becomes that much harder to change considerations about anything; and I mean *real* "change." If an individual really could freely change their considerations about existence as freely as they might like to think they can, then states of strong fragmentation would not exist and persist. And yet they do.

The purpose of systematic processing within the tradition of Mardukite Zuism & Metahuman Systemology is to increase free range of consideration available to the individual that is in command and control of their Human Condition as an Alpha Spirit. We have traveled down to this present state of affairs in the universe through an amazing journey—and this journey has indeed left us in a state of severe fragmentation; has left us fragmented about the identity of *Self*, and with absence of this knowledge or knowing, the true creative ability of the Spirit that has only been led to *consider* that these conditions of the physical universe are the absolute and everything. I am here to tell you that the physical universe—this *beta-existence*—that the Human Condition is presently anchored to, is but a speck of dust in the widest encompassing considerations of the ALL.

There is no reason for me to be unnecessarily esoteric here: each and every one of you carries a certain knowing that you have descended or "fallen" from some higher consideration of space-time energy and form—and just about every spiritual, philosophical and scientific methodology of the contemporary age seems to hint around a bit about this; but few of us are now content in waiting around to see what any further *agreement* with knowledge about the design of this physical beta universe is going to offer. Some of us have already peeked behind the screens and know what it is going to offer: a way of further dividing what is already here into another sub-level universe that the consideration of *I-as-Self* can get entrapped in.

The subject of *willingness* appears very frequently in our Systemology—and if we are going to think about things in terms of "magic" or "will" or "intention" and everything else along those lines, then this is the common meeting ground and a place to start; and it is why we consider this upper-route of Mardukite Metahuman Systemology as "Wizard" work; what some in *Piloting* courses have referred to as "Actualized Technicians." This is the work that is going to get us where we want to be—and there is no question about this.

The questions, at least for me, have always returned to organization and delivery, the means of structuring research and the way in which its discoveries are analyzed—all of which has occupied nearly a decade now of my current lifetime, just in regards to the Systemology that I have been involved in developing behind-the-scenes of the more publicly visible Mardukite *Grade-II* work and the "Routes" explored in *Grade-I*. These are excellent entrance points onto the *Pathway* so long as they are treated as such and not as the ends in themselves—which is too often the allure of those *Grades* and why they are allowed to be so freely explored in contemporary society: they are betting you will just get trapped in them.

By its very definition, "fragmentation" implies separation and disconnection; or what some define as dissonance, disharmony and discontinuity... a lot of "dis" words in there. It is for this reason that we emphasize "communication" at the very start of *Grade-IV*, because a *Seeker* is not going to get any further with their Master Grade material without some remedy of being very blatantly "out of communication" with *Life,* the *Universe* and whatever the individual is *unwilling* to "know," *unwilling* to "be" or "face" or "confront" and so on. A *Seeker* has narrowed their decisions of what is acceptable or conceivable to "know" or "be" within preexisting programming and has thus become an "effect" of the same, thereby giving up the responsibility for Self-determinism of the Alpha state.

This isn't a "fire and brimstone" sermon; I'm not here saying all this to judge or condemn; you have actually already accomplished that part on your own for yourself—and there is more value in my working to remedy that condition than there is in my reinforcing it as others have done in their methods of using knowledge and religion to further trap humanity in lower systems. We are all here now because we suddenly found ourselves *unwilling*—or believe ourselves *unworthy*—to consider any greater universe to occupy—and that, in a nutshell, defines the actual present state of affairs that we are treating in our Systemology.

The *Pathway of Fragmentation* that led us to this point did not happen all at once—nor is it important that you have a complete understanding of our full Cosmic History in order to deliver or receive effective processing. We are most concerned with what the *Seeker* is able to relate to most easily concerning *this* lifetime, before we begin to compound matters any further. We can already demonstrate the significance of these principles from *this* lifetime using the methods of *Analytical Recall* ("Route-2") and newer methods of *Communication Processing* ("Route-3"), which links circumstances and experiences to energetic flows that we refer to as "circuits" (in this manual).

When a *Seeker* is brought to consider the moments when they have gone out of communication in their life experiences, the realizations that may occur can be startling, but they are what we are concerned with. Of course, if we were to emphasize only the negative states and conditions we would only be effective in validating the negatives, which is only one type of flow. So, we may, for example, have the *Seeker* recall a time when they were in "good" communication in alternation with those times when they had broken ties or "cut" communication lines with others and yes, even "things"—really any "form" that we assign a label to and which can hold some kind of charge, and this is referred to as a "terminal."

Another excellent example to demonstrate to *Seekers* is what *willingness* has been diminished in connection—or rather "disconnection"—to certain *facets* that are emotionally charged or otherwise imprinted to restrict considerations. Each and every one of us has certain "charged" *places*, or *people* or *ideas* that trigger something —some kind of "ping"—just by their being flashed into our view. Sometimes we do not even need a physical representation of this to be present in our physical environment, but merely the thought or *concept* of it—being formed in our personal universe or as held in the "Mind's Eye"—puts us in a position to be "for" or "against" some mode of consideration. We are not even talking about "intuition" here, although it is sometimes mistaken as such when these channels aren't clear.

For example, an individual experiences some type of traumatic event or *Imprinting Incident* at such and such place and around such and such type of facets and suddenly the *willingness* for any later *duplication* of these is diminished. The individual doesn't even want to be around that physical area location any more and will even go to great lengths to avoid this "other-determined" restimulation that exposure incites. We've covered this stuff in *Grade-III* pretty well, especially in regards to the emotional encoding discussed in *The Tablets of Destiny* text. The point that was not necessarily driven home within that volume is that this successive validation of being "out of communication" with existence led the *Self* down a dark spiral of intentional forgetfulness; and this is a state that we are only now discovering any real remedies for after having swirled about within this murky mess for countless aeons.

When we talk about "communication," we often mean *willingness* to reach for *knowingness*. There is also the method of processing that we consider "objective," and this targets the *willingness* to reach for action and the command and control of *doing* things as cause. Yes, we must understand Cosmic Law or Causal Law, but it is not hard and certainly not as convoluted as physical sciences make it out to be. The average *Grade-II Mardukite* or Hermetic philosopher "understands" Cosmic Law pretty well—they have a handle on some of the basic principles by which beta-existence has been Ordered. And that's pretty good to know. But we are not trying to get entrapped any further into this Physical Universe and therefore do not need to make our sole occupation a discovery of more and more of its intricacies to agree with. It is, for the most part, a closed system with the illusion of recursive infinity so that it may become the sole occupation of its inhabitants; thereby infinitely divisible with "discovered knowledge," but nothing that will get you out of here.

The secret knowledge to mastering the worldly universe is what is "mastered" at the "Master" levels of our work, or rather the "*Master Grades.*" Most individuals who have come and gone never even reach the apex of *this* much during their lifetimes, then alone move past it. It is quite enamoring and it has been concisely condensed within our series of Master Edition hardcover volumes including: *The Great Magickal Arcanum, Merlyn's Complete Book of Druidism, Necronomicon: The Complete Anunnaki Legacy* and especially our *Grade-III* compendium, *The Systemology Handbook.*

I am often asked why the structure of the Mardukite Academy and Systemology School is designed as it is; why we concern ourselves with continued instruction of lower *Grade* work, for example, in ritual magic or Druidism at *Grade-I* in relation to Mardukite Zuism at *Grade-II*; or the pursuit of the mysteries of Mesopotamia to the extent that we do, even after discovering the heart and soul of a deeper Systemology once we began work with the *Tablets of Destiny*. There is no deception here: this work took a very long time to properly articulate. In order for any of this information to have value between us, realizations must be communicable: and so, here we are.

The *Pathway* that led us to this point is treacherous and tortuous, winding and spindling around all the corners of the globe and diverse culture populations that each brought their own spiritual and genetic memory to the timeline on planet Earth. As much as we are set out to de-sensitize or discharge more commonly known implanted terminals of the Human Condition, it should be observed that there are just as many—if not more—potential trappings when one crosses that first *Gate* and has stepped beyond mere considerations of mundane existence. This is when a lot of dissonance starts to occur and the ritual magician of the present age does not realize they are sitting in their circles talking to themselves, changing themselves or their considerations if effective; but more often than not, they are waiting for the *Bells, Books* and *Candles* to start talking *to them*, and well... we have already seen the personality effects that result from hanging suspended too long within that first sphere.

None of the lower Graded Routes are inherently wrong or bad in the moral or ethical sense. What they are—and what we have presented them as—are tiers on a very well-known ladder of ascent that lead us through the same barriers of consideration that we contributed in setting up for ourselves on the way here. This responsibility cannot be dismissed, else we have no actual authority or control over the matter. It is true we have given it up; have decided at one time or another that it would be better not to have it—but, now we know our mistake. The only issue, until fairly recently, is that there have been no successful demonstrations of a map to remedy this mistake. We've just sort of "lived with" it and agreed to it as it is (as its apparency would suggest in this beta-existence). They've just kept telling us to "suck it up" and "this is how it is" and we have agreed to be this effect via the very participation with this Game.

Handling of systematic processing—at Grade-IV—is codified by a schedule we developed, called: *Systemology Operating Procedure 2-C*, since it was introduced in *Liber-2C*, it is our second official outline of procedure, and is also a basic restoration of the Alpha Spirit's ability "to see." *SOP-2C* is a structured codification that includes and continues what we already set out with in *Grade-III*. The "Routes" that we've already considered *RR-SP* (or "*Route-1 Revised*" in *The Tablets of Destiny Revelation*) and "Analytical Recall" (*Route-2*) from *Crystal Clear* (*Liber-2B*) are still retained in *Grade-IV*, so make no mistake on their continued validity.

Willingness to "recall" and "resurface" and "remember"— the consideration that it is acceptable to *do so* without reservation—is where the *Seeker* arrives directly in *Grade-III*. At least, this is where we should expect them to arrive. If they aren't getting there on their own, and we are not going to leave them behind as a result, we simply incorporate *Grade-III* work as a preliminary to approaching the full extent of *Grade-IV*, and this newer development of *SOP-2C* allow for this. There is no reason that a *Seeker* cannot "self-process" themselves through the full extent of *Grade-III* work, either. The thing of it is: there is no side-stepping these processes and realizations. Without a free and total *willingness* for analytical recall on any aspect on an internal level, there can be no clear communication and certainly no demonstration of *Piloted* processing that will prove effective. We can process a *Seeker* to increase willingness for analytical recall and thereby improve their reach as communication, but until this whole matter is satisfactorily been resolved, there is no reason to even consider work of "higher" *Grades* and other "Routes." They will not prove to be as effective as they otherwise would be in the right hands or applications.

At *Grade-IV* we apply processing that directly targets energetic flow of communication and the *Seeker's* willingness to engage or reach as a *Self-directed* action—which again requires working through a whole host of energetic masses that have accumulated from heavily charged experiences; those that lay as a mass or resistance on an otherwise freely dispersing wire or energy current. If that seems too esoteric, let us just say that we must clear the obstacles that exist in the pathway of true *Self-honest* vision for the Alpha Spirit.

Fragmentation at this level of processing—particularly as it applies to the most readily available memory that we can resurface from this lifetime—is, at its core, entirely *analytical* or *mental* in nature. And by this, I mean that it is linked to the realm of "Thought." The fundamental inhibitions and excuses, the inabilities and hindrances we attach to our personality, the blocks and long lists of things we don't want to know or acknowledge—all of this accumulates over time, persisting to affect our range of present-time considerations and thoughts, based on fixed solidity of former considerations and thoughts; including those we have chosen to forget about and no longer take responsibility for. All of this contributed to where we consider *Self* to be; and all of this, once recognized and realized and accepted, becomes a map *out* of the mess we got ourselves into. All that is waiting, is for us to take the responsibility and resume command. That's it! That's all we have to do. But since we have so carefully and systematically arrived at this state we are at now, it seems it takes a bit more than a single strand of passive "positive thinking" to pull us completely out of its gravity. It shouldn't have to; though for the amount of fragmentation that most individuals are carrying around, it seems to take a little more work. But, I am pleased to say that: systematically, we *have* found a way, and that *is* the essence of our work now today.

METAHUMAN DESTINATIONS

— UNIT ONE —

MARDUKITE SYSTEMOLOGY
LIBER-2C

:: 1 ::
THE SYSTEMOLOGY OF COMMUNICATION

There is a chapter in *The Tablets of Destiny* (*Liber-One*) titled *"Communication of Thought, Will and Action on 'The Tablets of Destiny."* It describes activities and properties of "**ZU**" or *"Spiritual Life Energy"*—which is communicated through an entire series of **channels** and flowlines—but the actual systemology of "communication" may not be equally apparent to all *Seekers* from these descriptions. The *Systemology Society* realized that communication was the fundamental unifying key underlying all other action, motion and *Living* in systems.

In former presentations of *NexGen Systemology* composed a decade ago—such as the old *Reality Engineering*[*] lecture series—the concept of "communication" *was* defined in our earliest manuals as:

> "successful transmission of information, data or energy (&tc.) along a message line with a reception of feedback."

Of course this is a stable definition for some applications, but it deserves expansion for our "Pilot" course regarding the "control" of energy and power as it applies to higher-level understanding within Systemology. Therefore, we now also define "communication" as:

> "an energetic flow of intention to cause an effect (or duplication) at a distance; the personal energy moved or acted upon by will or else 'selective directed attention'; the 'messenger action' used to transmit and receive energy across a medium."

An individual consistently "interacts" with all manner of energies, information and forms in everyday life—including those found at more rigidly solid levels of the physical universe (or *beta existence*), but not limited to them. An

---

[*] See the appendix of the Grade-III *"Systemology Handbook."*

understanding of communication of *Awareness, Actualized Awareness* or *ZU-energy* is what allows *Self* to properly direct the relay of energy between "control centers" such as what is often very generally referred to as the "Mind" and "Body," which are systems controlled and commanded from a higher state of *spiritual beingness.*

When it comes to the individual—the *Alpha Spirit* as *Awareness or ZU*—communication involves all spiritual, psychological, emotional and physiological 'messenger actions' taking place along the "personal identity continuum" or Zu-line. This activity is essentially what many refer to as "**consciousness**" and it is a "communication of Awareness" relayed to and from various "control centers" **extant** on that *Spiritual Life Energy* **continuum.**

The "Standard Model of Systemology" (and Zu-line) demonstrates systematic communication of *Awareness* at any point between the continuity of physical solidarity in *beta-existence* and essentially *Infinity*. This workable "Standard Model" is explored quite extensively in *Grade-III Mardukite Systemology* material.*

Humans are prone to viewing communication exclusively in external or objective forms and mediums—such as speech or writing—but this is only one type of communication. However, in whatever manner we decide to view communication, it is an energetic "**flow**" of energy changing in space and this creates a cycle that in essence defines what we experience as "time." There is *no* treatment of time as an illusion within our systemology, because the observable cycles of energy, by their very nature, define "**time.**"

When an individual is experiencing "internal" (subjective) activity, this is a form of communication (energetic exchange, &tc.) that we can call "processing." An individual receives an incoming communication from the environ-

---

* Specifically *The Tablets of Destiny* (*Liber-One*) and *Crystal Clear* (*Liber-2B*) or the Grade-III *"Systemology Handbook."*

ment—or generates one internally—and then processes the energy as "information." This then "in-forms" or "forms-in" some kind of analytical significance for an individual; that is to say—it is given "consideration" or "meaning."

Knowledge concerning "influx" and "outflow" of communicable energy from the physical (beta) environment and the manner it is "processed" subjectively is now fully systematized for purposes of: study as *Self*, effective application to *Life*, and the establishment of "Professional Piloting Procedure." The beauty of "systemology" is that training on this subject remains consistent regardless of applications thereafter, because the basic data applies to all systems. When we consider specific qualities used to describe vibrant, radiant and charismatic individuals on Earth's **timeline** demonstrating an ability to *cause an effect* onto objective reality and the world-at-large, the common point to them all is the *ability to communicate.*

> —Communication is the primary means by which "personal fragmentation" takes place.
> —Systematic use of communication as "processing" is a primary means to "defragment" an individual.

Communication is potentially the most effective workable tool an individual may employ. Its proper handling means successful manifestation of will and intention to the highest level of cause; but improper control leads to becoming an effect, trapped by one's own **thought-forms**, **thought-habits** and reactive-responses automated by systems of the biochemical genetic organism an individual Alpha Spirit tends to identify as in space-time of *this* "beta existence."

There are many forms of communication that originate at higher levels of understanding or command of action, generated from a point of *Self* that is "exterior" to "beta-existence" as cause. This is also communicated through a series of personal (relay) channels (along the Zu-line) before an expression is manifested at another "level" of existence.

In most cases—where the origination or source-point of energy communication is Self-directed from the Alpha Spirit—the transmission of any current or flow of energy that carries an intention (or form) is treated as a **"thought-wave"** or "thought-vibration" in systemology.

Self has an incredible ability to use the **Mind-Systems** to generate and direct specific currents of energy which directly influence the experience of Reality in the Physical Universe. We know that thoughts *can* have a "reality" to them—and that the extent of this "reality" is equivalent to the strength of the original intention and clarity of the channel by which it is transmitted on.

Thoughts which manifest solidly enough for others to take a position, or "point-of-view" on, earn some quality of "reality" in the physical universe to the extent they may be communicated. This takes place even when an individual's point-of-view is *"against"* something; for there is now a "mass" or "solid" on that channel or flowline *to be* "against."

In *NexGen Systemology* it is just as important to understand how these "thought-waves" and "thought-forms" are communicated to create an effect on others as it is to realize the powerful effects our cycles of thought, belief, behavior and reaction have on us, working together to develop a particular "artificial beta **personality**" that we present to the world and which is the product of accumulated personal fragmentation and erroneous programming.

Success in the Game of Life is particularly dependent on the ability to communicate clearly not only with those other individuals and *Lifeforms* we interact with, but also with our Self, which is a state often referred to in *Mardukite Systemology* as *"Self-Honesty."* Our systematic method of achieving this as a basic beta-state is called *"The Pathway to Self-Honesty."*

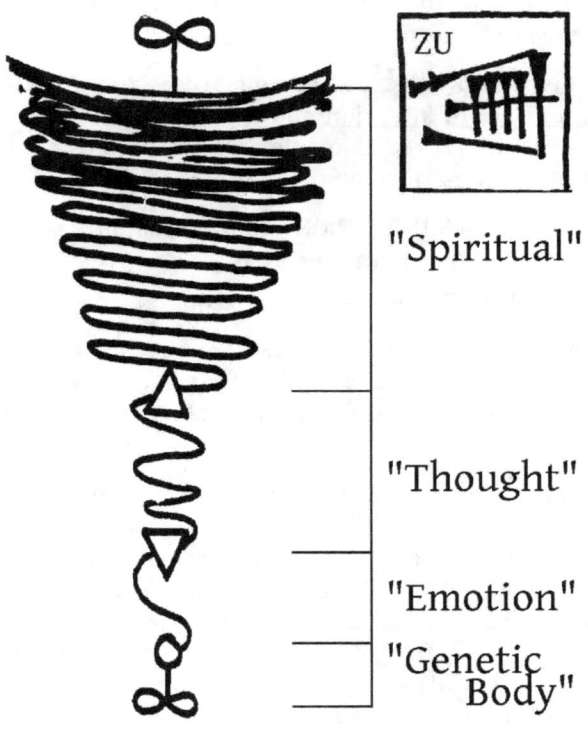

"Spiritual"

"Thought"

"Emotion"

"Genetic Body"

The functions of Communication exist in all facets and aspects experienced of *Life, the Universe and Everything*. When we consider the spiritual, religious and mystical applications of communication throughout history, there is no shortage of examples wherein the human population has made attempts—however successful—at reaching toward the Infinite, which is otherwise considered some kind or another type of "communication with God."

We find practical applications of communication in any effort or intent to "make something known" or "bring to light" what is otherwise unknown or not treated as presently existing. We find interchange of "thought energy" taking place wherever "**knowledge** is imparted" or a medium is used to share in or partake in the transmission of energy or "information."

There are two basic components that correspond with communication: intention and attention. These are comparable to the Three Principle Systems of "Cosmic Manifestation" as described on the "Arcane Tablets"—*

COMMUNICATION—"Motion/action".

INTENTION—"Substance/form"

ATTENTION—"Awareness/consciousness"

Those continuing their studies from Grade-III would be most familiar with the concept of Intention as an application or active property of the WILL at (5.0) on the Standard Model.

> intention : to intend, have "in Mind" or signify (give significance to) for or toward a particular purpose; in Systemology (from the Standard Model)—the spiritual activity at WILL (5.0) directed by an Alpha Spirit (7.0); the application of WILL as "Cause" from a higher order of Alpha Thought and consideration (6.0), which then may continue to relay communications as an "effect" in the universe.

When we consider the act of attending with our presence, the direction of focus for Awareness could very well be toward a specific aspect or thing. There are, however, a few more components to this activity.

> attention : active use of Awareness toward a specific aspect or thing; the act of "attending" with the presence of Self; a direction of focus or concentration of Awareness along a particular channel or conduit or toward a particular terminal node or communication termination point; the Self-directed concentration of personal energy as a combination of observation, thought-waves and **consideration.**

---

* Refer to "The Tablets of Destiny Revelation" (Liber-One).

Communication is a systematic process by which an intention is given attention; the intention is projected by a sender or source-point and given some quality of attention by a receiver or receipt-point where it is treated as an effect. The cyclic action actually creates and defines space and time as it is occurring.

Whether treated as an interpersonal exchange among human bodies or between universes, the nature of a communication defines the range or boundaries (**parameters**) of the relationship between any two "things"—or "system terminals." On a purely systematic level, communication is a flow of energy between two terminals (terminations or end points): one projecting and one receiving. When communication is "two-way," when

it is flowing in both directions, a "**circuit**" or "cycle of actions" has formed.

INTENTION → ATTENTION
(Directing Attention) → (Accepting Intention)

Where communication appears in any system on any level, it is treated as a pathway, bridge, conduit, gateway or channel between two "points." Quality of any two-way circuit of communication is defined by clarity of transmission and its ability to relay clearly across a proximity (distance of space) or between terminals. The "Standard Model of Systemology" demonstrates how all existence—*Life, the Universe and Everything*—is a composite system of intricate "two-way" pathways all acting together "systematically" as one whole, but composed of parts (or "sub-systems").

NexGen Systemology is the result of thousands of years of research and experimentation concerning the highest ideal state of Knowing and Being—the most effective efforts toward Self-Actualization and freeing the innate power and identity of the Spirit. It should come as no surprise for us to then treat the nature of existence as a "communication of energies" or "energy flows" taking place between all points and "terminals" in existence as an intricate "web-like matrix."

Communication terminals (or "nodes") within a functional system—even a "living" one—are not restricted only to other *Lifeforms*. Anything that has been put forth as an "intention" into existence is given a sense of "being" and "form" when it is permitted *to be*. And this *beingness* is the result of "attention" on the "intention" enough to validate "it exists."

Fragmentation of any kind is a distortion that inhibits free flow of energy (or clear communication) and the understanding (comprehension) or duplication of the energy received as an effect. An individual also maintains a chronic level of *Self-Honesty* and *Actualized Awareness* (experienced as the "freedom of the Spirit") equivalent to the degree that their "lines" of communication for experience with various terminals are "free and clear."

The goals of "systemology education," "systematic processing" and "piloted procedures" are all to assist the *Seeker* to free the restrictions and barriers erroneously agreed to on communication lines and thereby "defragment" the flow of energy. An individual is principally as **"capable"** as they are freely able to clearly communicate *Self-expression*. Effective "systematic processing" is heavily dependent on successfully managing these flows.

:: 2 ::
THE CONTROL OF COMMUNICATION SYSTEMS

Thoughts, just like other forms of energy and matter, are "waves" or "wave-forms" that carry the cosmic property of communication: *motion*. A "wave" is a messenger action (or *'motion'*), carrying a "point" of some type or degree to another "point" across a distance, and therefore changing "space." Rate of transmission across space defines "time." We often express a "wave-action" with considerations of "time" as "vibration" and "frequency." This is a "measured observation" of "time" between "points" in "space"—which is to say "communication of Reality."

"Clear communication" or "clear channels" of energy transmission, mean a "duplication with certainty" of a message or energy flow. Without such "understanding," what many pass off as "communication" is really only "distortion" and noise—erroneous fragmentation promoting "turbulence" of an energy flow.

> turbulence : a quality or state of distortion or disturbance that creates irregularity of a flow or pattern; the quality or state of aberration on a line (such as ragged edges) or the emotional "turbulent feelings" attached to a particular flow or terminal node; a violent, haphazard or disharmonious commotion (such as in the ebb of gusts and lulls of wind action).

The common expression in *Systemology* for clear relay of communication, between *Self* and the universe, is "*A-for-A.*" This means a relay or projection of energy, information or thought—as "A"—is directly and perfectly duplicated with the same "intention and meaning" at its receipt-point—as "A."

When an individual's attention is directed or focused on some specific bit of incoming energy (therefore becoming a receipt-point of energy/information), the information comes in on an attention line and given significance and meaning based on either a *Self-Honest* experience or based on associative data collected from the past.

"Associative knowledge" is often times quite solid as a "thoughtform" or "mental image" which manifests and solidifies along energetic channels of experience quite literally as "beliefs" about Reality. Rigid solid beliefs, particularly at lower levels of realization, automate the "significance" assigned to any reception of energy and its related experience. *Self* (as Observer) is not able to "see" past these artificial solids, filters and screens, which creates turbulence on the pathway of what should otherwise be a clear communication of Will and Intention between *Alpha* and *Beta* states—between the Alpha-Thought of the Alpha Spirit and the control maintained over the beta-form that it operates and monitors.

In *Grade-III*, the *"Pathway to Self-Honesty"* is described as a journey of clearing spiritual energy channels of debris and erroneous associations imprinted by the environment—those entwined and solidified energies inhibiting total experience as an actualized *Self*. The *"practicum"* of *Grade-IV* employs *"Professional Piloting Procedure"* to engage two-way communication flows between a *Pilot* and *Seeker* in order to manage turbulence on lines directed toward terminals or terminations (objects, ideas, events, memories) which otherwise do not "talk" or "respond" and which result in no systematic repair on their own.

Once fixed in place, an individual is likely to keep hitting such fragmentation as a "barrier" to communication of true *Self-Honest* reality experience unless properly managed. The significance cannot be overemphasized: experience of *Life* is a communication between *Self* and a *Universe*.

The greater a *Seeker's* true understanding about *Life, the Universe and Everything,* the more certain and willing they are to project communications; which in turn is an increased ability to manage the "personal environment." We can be certain that in all of its creative expressions, the responsibility and capability attached to the true nature of the Alpha Spirit as a "being" is to *create, experience, know*—all of which is based in the personal control of communication.[*]

A specific channel by which an individual manages control of the communication line as Self, is described and demonstrated in *Grade-III* materials as the *"Zu-line."* Clear communication and control is only possible by a "clear pathway" between relay points on the *"Zu-line"*—a "straight line" of energetic communication on the Standard Model, between the Alpha Spirit at (7.0) and continuity of the "physical universe" as *beta existence*. There are other relay points on this channel while an Alpha Spirit controls a genetic body—meaning many points at which *fragmentation* may occur and an intention is later diverted by some other crooked or jagged wave-form that provides distortion in the follow through of a communication to be accurately duplicated A-for-A. Fragmentation is what inhibits the clear passage of communication and therefore its control.

Many communication circuits exist on the *"Zu-line"* (Standard Model). Any of these may store erroneous or misguided personal **"charge"** as fragmentation. When not resolved, this state of fragmentation generally increases over time and even through many lifetimes. To begin: we can productively concern ourselves with inhibition to communicate and improper management of control experienced in *this* lifetime. As more emotional turbulence, painful experience and intellectual programmed **dissonance** accumulates as *fragmentation*, an individual falls out of communication with the physical body, the physical universe and then finds considerable uncertainty in any "sense" of *Self* remaining.

Personal fragmentation is significantly responsible for a general inhibition to express communication efficiently

---

[*] *"To see, to study and to experience all things."* (Druid Triad)

"at WILL"—which is to say at (5.0) on down through the ZU-line on the Standard Model. An individual is very heavily fragmented during their existence and this is a state that may be repaired and rehabilitated by systematic piloted methods on a gradient scale—until, of course, a *Seeker* has recovered enough personal certainty to *actually* change their state and "Mind" with the power of a single consideration or realization on their own.

At every level or definition it may be stated that all abilities of the Alpha Spirit may be reduced to one kind of another of communication—between *Self* and some other "point" or "termination" for our attention. Even if its nature is entirely created by and for *Self*, the "point" still acts as a systematic "terminal" one can therefore "reach toward" or "move away from" or have some other kind of communicative exchange with as a "form." The fact that an individual *takes perceived stimuli* and *then creates their own* mental images of reality to perceive and communicate with is generally demonstrated in *NexGen Systemology*.

An individual's chronic state of inhibition regarding communication is often the result of many reoccurring "breaks" "interruptions" or "barriers" encountered in previous efforts. It is even possible that an individual has received authoritarian encoding regarding either the "demands" for communication, and/or a "punishment" is enforced as a consequence when one does. This encoding remains as fragmentation and may greatly affect all future attempts—the very willingness—to communicate.

An individual decides to "shut off" the flow of communication with a particular aspect, thing, thought, or terminal-node as opposed to properly managing the flow. This may generate "automated mechanisms" that similarly treat more and more of these flows outside of Self-determinism. These are the first considerations that create defining "walls" that limit personal willingness and clear view of existence.

When we consider strong lingering *fragmenting* effects of communication and our relationship with the environment: it is often *what we did not say* or *the answers we did not receive* that cause us to still energetically "hang on" to these lines or anchor points with part of our attention thereafter.

This attention—and generation of any reality on its channel—will be fragmented. This type of fragmentation is reinforced by "internal communications" with an individual's own personal "interior" systems. Very often these flows of attention are directed toward mental walls and screens used as a substitute terminal-node in place of the actual objects, life-forms, &tc. When a stimulus presents, the individual projects images treated as reality "within the mind" and then proceeds to interact with them, playing out and reacting with all manners of fragmented considerations.

You may have witnessed—or even yourself experienced—how internal circuitry with such fragmentation can "work a person up" or "down" or get them "spun" on some particular aspect. Humans can cause themselves sickness and ranges of anxiety with no other outside influence but their own internal considerations of fragmented communication. The Standard Model suggests that Cosmic Spiritual Life Energy ("Zu") comes into and flows through the Alpha Spirit from Infinity as a continuous and essentially unlimited "inflow." This being the case, the only matters that have detrimental affects on the Spirit's experience of *Life, the Universe and Everything*, would be those places, points, circuits and flows where energy is restricted, fragmented or otherwise blocked.

If energy is flowing in at a constant, then any energetic barriers, imprints, considerations of limited belief, emotional response-reactive charges on "mental images"—or any other blockage—*will* build up pressure and concentrate free energy as more solid masses. All systems are composed of interchanges and interactions, flow-lines and actions—and they are **dynamic** in that each level is affected by and/or affects other levels...systematically. All personal systems and universal systems operate on energetic principles—no matter what terminology is used to define them. For this reason, all of the most paramount lessons of the magician, mystic, spiritualist or systemologist concern ENERGY.

Many factors lead to a *Seeker's* sense of communication fragmentation—some easier to process or more quickly recalled in analytical sessions than others. Most involve encounters with perceived barriers or improper external control (and authoritarian enforcement), but all of them affect willingness of an individual to generate or communicate a creation, even as simple as a single thought.

The human condition—and even considerations of the Alpha Spirit—essentially evolve out of a sequence of observations that lead to what an individual is or isn't willing to communicate freely with, and therefore be a part of as a responsible creator or *Self-determined* being. Each time an individual is blocked from extending their reach, they are less willing to "speak up" or "engage" thereafter. This does not generally happen all at once; unless there is a very serious heavily charged incident far back on the spiritual timeline.

Beta existence is among the lowest levels of cosmic communication—ideals and intentions readily as solid as billiard balls banging against one another and reconfirming the heavy solidity of a condensed universe. That is the truth of *this* universe; there is no illusion about that. The only *holograph* is the one projected in the mind—turning the energies and waves we place attention on into definable solids and forms with meaning and significance when we duplicate its imagery in our mind as "Reality." We are always interacting with reality and the universe in proportion to the clarity that we duplicate in the mind (A-for-A) the clear or true nature of the "inflow." Response-reaction mechanisms and associative identifications evolve based on how "images" in the mind are treated and communicated with in the past and not as the product of a present environment.

Being "out of communication" or "out of touch" is a result of too limited of consideration, responsibility and willingness to be *Self-directed*. It is constrictive and limiting insofar as it defines or dictates the free range of *Self*. The more places we are unwilling to go; the more people we are unwilling to talk to; these begin to define stringent limitations when an individual identifies *Self* with a physical form that may be so easily entrapped through automated mechanisms. That which we dislike or want to avoid; what we disagree with or attempt to reduce the reality of; the entire idea of what we are willing to keep close to us in proximity—these are all matters of consideration that are either given a free span of accessibility or else are limited to associative fragmentation, which at the lowest forms of human experience seem very much attached to "reactive emotional charges" on the images we conjure to mind every day.

A *Seeker* or *systemologist* that has completed *Grade-III* materials (that are the literal foundation for the present work) and is familiar with the Standard Model, should come to the realization that: communication is an exercise or expression of *Self* as Will and Intention—which may be directed fully from *Self* at cause from an *Alpha* point "exterior" to the physical universe (*beta*); however, its expression is managed by the "*Master Control Center*" (MCC or "Mind Systems")—and potentially the "*Reactive Control Center*" (RCC or "Emotional Response")—when the genetic vehicle or physical form is used as the catalyst to communicate this Will and Intention with the universe.

:: 3 ::
COMMUNICATION AND PILOTING AS A GAME

As an intellectual pursuit and field of applied spiritual philosophy, *NexGen Systemology* is notoriously connected to two basic preexisting studies that developed strongly during the past century: "systems theory" and **"games theory"**—of which are treated only with the highest-level mathematical jargon in all approaches outside of *NexGen Systemology*.

"If we consider the Physical Universe we are experiencing as a 'game-board' on a table, then the table, the chairs, the manner of the room in which they sit...none of this is 'in play' or in any way existing within the parameters of the game itself. Other than, of course, at a higher level, someone choosing to manufacture the game and the Alpha-players choosing to play it, there is no existential correlation between 'Dimensions.' From *within* the game we cannot ascertain anything about some other all-encompassing environment directly, although we are certain that whatever the 'I' is, it must occupy this other space with its spiritual existence and then project its Awareness and Will into this Game as Life."   —The Tablets of Destiny (Liber-One)

"The higher states that we achieve result in higher complexities of the System we are in. It just works out that way. We tend to equate it best to 'game theory' at this juncture because we are talking about systematic variables that, yes, are governed by Law, but we cannot apply this Law directly to the true force that is doing the determining of action—and that is the Self. The Self is making choices."   —The Tablets of Destiny (Liber-One)

"The paramount signature Game of the actualized Alpha Spirit is an ability to create and un-create at Will. At every turn in Systemology we find increasing realization of abilities and education regarding applications of <u>Games</u> and Systems to the management of our beta-existence and our environment— and every step of the way we are working **successively** toward the Actualization of the Alpha Spirit as 'I' of Self. All of these aspects, conditions—and even the very Processes themselves—point toward one key theme: CONTROL."   —Crystal Clear (2B)

An individual is probably already familiar with the idea of "games"—especially in the sense of "competitive sports." At basic: a "game" is "any strategic situation where the power of choice is employed or affected." We then refer to individuals in the game as "players" if they are "an individual that is making decisions in a game and/or is affected by decisions others are making in the game, especially if those other-determined decisions now affect the possible choices."

In establishing the "game" and "players" we discover what some call "common knowledge," which is to say the facts that all "players" know, and they know that all other "players" also know. One might assume that the very structure of the "game" shared between players is a "common knowledge"—though this does not appear to be shared equally as true *Awareness* among all players of the Game of Life. This immediately creates another condition for players to consider, which is also treated by Game Theory: "Rationality."

"Rationality" is the extent to which a player seeks to play the game—make decisions, &tc.—in order to maximize gains (or else survival conditions) achievable within the parameters of any given game. In *NexGen Systemology*, we extend this definition to describe "the ability and willingness of an individual to reach toward conditions that promote the highest level of survival and existence and thereby make the best choices and moves to see the desired goal manifest."

When Game Theory is applied to Life, it demonstrates very clearly that "power of choice" is only as free as an individual is able to consider all choices. At high levels, the Game of Life, Universes and Everything is demonstrable with precision logic and affected directly by Alpha Thought; so then why aren't these same realizations accessible to the average person today? Well, they are. However, most individuals no longer carry a free range of consideration with them as a spiritual truth and instead have begun to think purely in terms of mechanistic qualities inherent in the low-energy condensed **continuity** of the physical universe.

Understanding the "power of choice" has been a constant staple of the social sciences and is even of significant interest to a *Seeker* as they work their way on the *Pathway to Self-Honesty* and beyond. Modern esoteric interest in these matters is even as antiquated as the academic pursuits—to which we find significant increase of attention being given to "systems theory" and "games theory" as society moved through the 1900's. Nearly all contributors to these fields during the 20th century were highly educated mathematicians.

Systemologists look for many ways to demonstrate objective truths. In fact, processes are developed so that a *Seeker* may experience principles of truth demonstrated with as much significance of "reality" as their former fragmentation has been instilled. After an individual has already accepted or "agreed" to a particular statement or barrier of reality, they put up another fact or statement or solid **postulate** against it; and confusion often ensues.

We refer to "Piloting" and "Processing" in *NexGen Systemology* as a form of "two-person cooperative game"—which is a concept formally developed by John Nash in 1950. "Piloting" would be a "game"; it involves "two persons" and is "cooperatively" engaged specifically for overall improvement (gain). A "Piloted Session," by definition, is a formal interactive situation that follows a model; and much like other games, it involves more than one player. Otherwise, a game with only one player is usually called a "decision problem"—and we can be assured that *Seekers* already have much practice playing at that one, with all of the fragmentary free-association and loop-patterns that tends to result from operating states outside Self-Honesty.

John Nash (a famous mathematician) explained that "a game is 'non-cooperative' if it is impossible for the players to communicate or collaborate in any way" and that players in a two-person cooperative game are "not 100% opposed; but not 100% coincident." They are not necessarily a "team" in the truest game-sense of the word; but they are both invested in or have their interests in the mutually beneficial results that ensue. Since we are not earning our "gains" through conflict, the "two-person game" of "processing" is, however, 100% cooperative.

As a cooperative game between two people, the most powerful strategies toward sharing a reality and presence, discussing and agreeing on a plan of action for sessions, and then actually conduct processing sessions to any notable gain...all utilizes "two-way communication."

The "Game of Processing" is carried out between two "players"—a "Pilot" and a "Seeker." It is the "Pilot" that is responsible for managing and handling the *flight*—which is to say, the "session." The "Professional Pilot" is trained and experienced to manage the environment and processing of a session as a means of assisting the *Seeker* in reaching a destination; which in most instances is a general increase in the *Seeker's* chronic state of *Being* and *Knowing.*

A "session" is all aspects/facets concerning a "session." The environmental setting; the focus or presence (set) of the *Seeker*; the methods or techniques used in practice by the Pilot—these are all considered a part of the "session" as a 'game-field'. This is to say: the agreed upon reality between players for a space and time in which to play a game. This is no dissimilar to the concept of a mystical microcosmic playing field, 'sacred space' or 'ritual area' as desired.

A Pilot may be said to employ both "two-way communications" and **"processing command lines"** (or PCLs)—yet even the "command lines" are transformed back into a "two-way" flow with proper use of **"acknowledgment"** and "communication processing." For a *Seeker* to communicate freely in session they must feel safe and uninhibited to do so, which a Pilot must assist. The purpose is not to have a *Seeker* merely talk endlessly over the course of a session—because such would render no gain at all—but the *Seeker* must be fully present in session and willing to participate in the game.

Systemology presents a Game of Self-Actualization. If a *Seeker* wishes to play a different game, or wishes to be in some way intentionally difficult or unwilling as some other misguided personal exercise, it is only their own loss. We will assume (in this manual) that a *Seeker* is a systemologist that at least understands something of what is expected of them—in terms of compliance and cooperation—in order to participate in an effective session that produces real spiritual gains. The entire purpose of the session is to increase the *Seeker's* certainty of ability and sense of knowing and being—in spite of any greater higher-view interests the Pilot may have for "serving the betterment of society" or the esteem of "certifying an A.T. Actualized Technician" &tc. Any success the Pilot has toward "greater" goals is dependent wholly on actual gains achieved by the *Seeker* they are in "communication and control" with.

Discipline of the Pilot is a primary concern at this juncture of *"Flight School."* Just as a *Seeker* must be encouraged and ensured that they are in a safe environment (and among safe company) to produce necessary communications (and arrive at any "self-realization" on one's own), a Pilot requires practice maintaining a non-reactive state in the presence of a *Seeker*. That is to say: the Pilot is able to meet (confront/face) any encounter or communication with the *Seeker* in session without exhibiting or displaying an emotional response-reaction. This is practiced with precision as part of "Pilot Training." It is also important for Pilots to practice methods of "two-way communication" demonstrated within this manual.

This handbook is prepared as a result of carefully researched experiments and trials conducted in person—either by the present author directly, or via long-standing elite systemologists. In any case, instruction and research were inseparable to culminating any objective presentation as a book—especially one that might allow for understanding and use of this technology outside or independent of direct supervision and input from the present author.

There are many reasons a Pilot should seek to control their own reactive-response mechanisms, but when it comes to piloting a "*systematic session*," then high-level Self-control must be demonstrated to a *Seeker* at all times. For example: while running a process during a session, the *Seeker* may begin to produce any number of personal realizations. These are "acknowledged" in live communication and recorded in a "Flight-log"* without necessarily having to "certify the truth" of the received communication, neither dismissing or adding data to validate anything further on the "comm line." In other words, this is not the time for a Pilot to start bringing up personal anecdotes about some time or instance when they thought about such and such or that such and such happened to them. That's what classrooms are for.

A Pilot must be uninhibited in their willingness and ability to *listen* in spite of the actualized level of a *Seeker*. Likewise, the *Seeker* will naturally gain greater confidence with the Pilot and with the application of practices as more time is spent in session together. This "familiarity" seems to have a positive impact with producing greater levels of commu-

---

* Also available: *Systemology Truth Seeker's Adventure Journal.*

nication and thereby increasing the potential gains for higher-level processing.

Most methods developed for *Grade-IV Systemology "Professional Piloting Procedure"* are based on years of "energy-work" and "esoteric experiments" regarding "communication with the physical universe." Until full certainty of Will and Intention is returned to the Alpha Spirit —whereby a *Seeker's* consideration of one thing or another can actually be changed with Alpha Thought and free of emotional reactivity—the caliber of work alluded to throughout this manual is particularly more challenging to manage directly as "self-processing" (speaking to those who are previously familiar with the *"Crystal Clear"* text).

In some cases, elementary self-processing was found to promote additional circuitry in some individuals that are likely to "hold on tightly" to their heavily charged "mental images" and set up terminals for additional "internal communication" or "self-talk" long after the session has ended; long after any function or purpose of a mental image had expired. When a *Seeker* does not (or cannot sanely) differentiate between the level of reality (or state of agreements) of the internal subjective from the external objective communications with the physical universe, all manners of fragmentation likely will ensue. Systemology processing simply assists an individual put "phases" and "identities" of various universes in line with one another.

Whether a Pilot or *Seeker*, the effective purpose behind the *Grade-IV* course on "control and communication" is to establish a state of uninhibited willingness to communicate on clear channels. This is one primary aspect to rehabilitating or regaining the higher faculties of the "Mind and Spirit." This often involves analyzing deeply laden postulates or barriers that restrict what and with whom we communicate for fear of invalidation, error, loss or pain.

:: 4 ::
FUNDAMENTALS OF COMMUNICATION
FOR NEXGEN SYSTEMOLOGY

Clear understanding of the subject of communication is a benefit to all individuals—yet it is of particular interest to systemologists, *Seekers* and Pilots. In *"The Tablets of Destiny"* textbook, "Levels of Understanding" are defined based on the general "grade" that a knowledge base is collected and how data is organized and evaluated. There are many levels of consideration or significance; and each relatively defines similarities and differences.

"Understanding" is: a clear 'A-for-A' duplication of a communication as 'knowledge', which may be comprehended and retained with its significance assigned in relation to other 'knowledge'. This means that personal experience of an event, static piece of writing or the information relayed in speech (*&tc.*) is rarely given the same 'significances' by all Observers—nor is the presentation of true knowledge of *Life, the Universe and Everything* treated with the same degree of understanding by all individuals maintaining a relationship with the human condition.

It is for this reason that true understanding—which is to say *actual realization*—cannot be enforced, instructed or even demonstrated with simple language to those who are not yet in a position (or willing to put themselves in a position) to be a receipt-point for a true A-for-A understanding. This very fundamental prompted such esoteric axioms as: "the lips of wisdom are sealed except to ears of understanding" or "when the student is ready, the teacher appears."

We then may describe the exact relay and duplication of a communication or knowledge as:

$$A\text{-for-}A$$
$$A = A \; ; B = B \; ...$$
$$A \rightarrow A$$

In technical terms, we could even treat communication as a teleportation between points. But—what about fragmented knowledge manifestations? Imprints? Etc.?

B=A; C=A; D=A ... (differences are generalized as similar; all *facets* equal "A")

A=B; A=C; A=D ... (similarity is erroneously distinguished as something different)

Elsewhere this is defined as "**dissonance**."

In *NexGen Systemology*, the nature of communication and nature of energy flows are essentially synonymous studies. We are treating a systematic relay of energy as a communication; whether we are engaging our attention across a room for a piloted session or across the veils of cosmic existence: the fixing in place of a thought, will or intention as cause or as a source-point and transmitting it clearly across energetic channels *is* the very action of all *Life, the Universe and Everything* in communication with all *Life, the Universe and Everything.*

Even when we are not engaged in formal "two-way communication" (by which we may directly receive positive feedback and acknowledgment about reception and comprehension of a message), the purpose of any origination, creation, message or communication *is* for it *to be* received. "One-way" flows are simply communications for which no answer has been sent back as an acknowledgment or response, which can also manifest as a *compulsion* to communicate.

A Pilot may be surprised to discover just how many individuals have energy held up in their life still waiting for a "response" on some line. And far too often, an individual following standard issue human programming fails to differentiate the inert continuity of the physical universe from the "living beings" also identified with some kind of energy-matter system or "physical body."

Beta-Existence is not a "living form"—and it tends to only communicate on the lowest-levels and these are among the most solid that we know of. When we *push*; it *pushes* back. We have already, at this level, come to think of it as a some thing to push against and therefore validate its solidity. It is composed therefore entirely of solids far more condensed and compacted then any of the upper levels from which this debris has clearly settled from.

Communications of thought, intention—any energy, &tc.—are all transmitted or projected from a source-point and they create a certain space-time around them that carries potentially observed qualities. There must be some "thing" to be sent and received. It must occupy a unique space and by passage through any medium, may be defined in terms of time. This means that at upper levels: space-time energy-matter may all be *created* with Alpha Thought.

The channel of communication may be direct, but it also has many relay points, even within the most basic form of expression. The Cause-Point (Sender) intends "A"; the Comm Line travels across space (Messenger Action) as "A"; received by a Receipt-Point (Node or Terminal) as "A"; and finally results, or is comprehended, at the Effect-Point as "A."

"Fragmentation" and "distortion" are words describing "absence of clarity" in a message or communication. Whatever has been fed in on the "line" is not being processed in the same way across all distances. Of course, a greater likelihood for a distorted communication exists the greater the distances, the greater the number of relay points (or points of "duplication"), the greater the perceived barriers to divert, and thus the greater the communication lag or "time" between relay points.

Fragmentation is generally a consequence of "associations" and "significances" assigned as a meaning to any facet, concept—whatever "A" actually *is*. And therein lies the issue for many individuals in differentiating "A" not as an "A"—or what has been instructed or emotionally encoded to mean "A"—but as an actual *is*. If something *is*, then we consider it *real*, but only then. Therefore, we can only communicate "reality" or "what *is* real" to the extent that it is able to be exchanged—both sent and received—across a distance between two points as an *is*. The degree of understanding as shared communicable reality with any "terminal **node**" (anything that may be distinguished as an *is*, and therefore as a 'termination point' of a system) is said to be the degree to which one is "in" or "out" *of communication* with said 'point'.

Proper relay of clear communication is very important for the optimum continuation of all life, but is also particularly important on a formal technical level in *Professional Piloting Procedure* and even upper-level work. As it is the key to remedy and realize all other stations along the *Pathway to Self-Honesty*, the repair of "personal communication" is where most assistance begins, because without it there can be no higher-level work; this is to say that the higher-level work in no way substitutes what is intended to be earned at subsequent *Grades*.

There is an illusion by many not properly initiated into the folds of the Ancient Mystery School, that somehow, the "higher Grades" are "higher" in their superiority or power to the "lesser" ones—and yet as one works through a properly graded scale, one does not actually notice much greater of an incline or increase in the next tier than the former. There is an illusion that if one could simply gaze upon the words of some higher order of knowledge, with the symbols arranged in just such and such an order, than an explosion of effect will instantaneously occur and the *Seeker* will immediately sprout wings and catapult them entirely out of any consideration of the material cosmos and back into a state of Alpha cause.

However, the likelihood or "quantum probability" that such phenomenon is to occur is low. It is not impossible. In fact, if anything, it is a semblance or memory of a former time of spiritual actualization when the Self was very much in control of its own directed energies and in the clearest and strongest modes of Self-determinism, even while monitoring a "body."

This type of phenomenon is, of course, not what we are claiming to reproduce with a pursuit of the *Pathway to Self-Honesty* via methods given as "*NexGen Systemology*"—since ours is a methodology systematically **graded** to provide no sharp peaks or drop offs for those that wish to follow the map. Of course, the more we wish to push away, the more space is created and thus we have the illusion of a perpetually 'expanding' physical universe solely due to the solidity of the considerations taking place at these lower-level concentrations.

It is the consideration of "distance" that we will treat next, because for some this is only thought of in terms of literal spatial distance—and this is fine, so long as one adds to their consideration of "distance" the association of the willingness to have something "close" or "far" in proximity. This means that on a communication level, the distance is equivalent to our literal proximity but also our willingness to allow some 'thing' to come "close" to us.

We use these terms very specifically because obviously a person could be standing right in front of you but still be refusing to listen or be a receipt-point because they don't *like* you—or they have some other associative fragmentation connected with the kind of "terminal" you represent —they could be said to be "at a distance" or "out of communication." And when this behavior is enacted intentionally, or is noticed between individuals, or is stated in conversations related to the same, humans generally are aware that in spite of physical locales attributed to space, an individual is in fact "distancing" themselves—at least energetically.

It is also noticed that this "distance" can be reduced with "interest" and "agreement"—and then suddenly individuals are in energetic proximity to be in communication. The state of agreement and interest leads to a shared reality from which additional attention may be applied on the communication line. It is only after this "distance" is bridged that any productive "two-way communication" can ensue.

An individual will keep that which they *like* (or feels *familiarity* or fond *emotional ties*) in closer communication than what they do not *like* or *agree* with. Hence they have no real understanding of whatever is "not liked" and therefore continue to exercise no real *Self-directed* control toward it on those energetic comm-lines. These may become metaphoric "walls" and "imprints" that add to the "distancing" factor of clear communications.

One of the issues for the Alpha Spirit that is a creative force outside beta-existence is that it is identifying with control centers (for a form) that are very much anchored in the physical universe. Of course, this is not the only potential existence for a Spirit—but it does come to believe so as it starts to associate more and more with the solidity of the physical body and both the considerations and restrictions associated with the physical universe.

A *Seeker* must actualize a realization—through processing —that objects and walls found in the physical universe are a solidification, result or effect from concentrations of thought-energy or attention applied to give these things there solid forms. They aren't living terminals and they do not communicate. They have only the significance of being a solid; an inert part of physical continuity that are an *is* only because someone has assigned an existence to it.

At this (0.0) level of solidity of largely gathered particle masses, billiard balls and concrete walls, it requires something of equal solidity to even communicate with it—and for this the human condition is given a standard-issue array of sensory inputs in which to receive data from the environment as assigned to a "physical body."

Our level of communication projected as a willingness to reach from a room might be limited to feeling the solidity of the surrounding barrier-walls by touch—and so we know that they are there for the body, and we are even in control of the body as we direct its motions to do this. But we are also aware that there is a higher truer and more eternal part of us—the actual "I" that was never *in* the body in the first place, and need not be restricted to walls.

Communication in the physical universe can involve any perceptual channel that the genetic vehicle (organic organism) has the faculties for. There is already a wide range of energies and motions taking place around us—but we must have an appropriate type of "terminal" or "receiver" that operates along a level to communicate with it; even if it is only to receive the impressions of a communication at the effect-point.

The basic energies are already in existence, but when we "tap those wires" and put any attention in the directions of their flows, we are "aware" that something is taking place. We selectively use the word "awareness" in instances of actualized knowingness and beingness because it denotes that there is a range or field of "unawareness" just by the consideration. Therefore, what we are "unaware" of is no less true or extant or an *is* on an objective level than it otherwise would be—the difference is what is brought within the realm of control or the proximity of reach in order to share responsibility in it. Control without responsibility is simply *enforcement*; and it is generally to this lesser level of awareness that most systems are brought in the absence of responsible control.

When an individual opens up channels of communication —any type of communication—they are essentially directing attention along a "flow-line." This "flow-line" could be systematically demonstrated in various states with various wave-form graphics, but what is most important or critical to us for practical purposes is simply whether the line is heavily charged with fragmentation *or* not.

In systemology, we treat all projections (or radiations) from a point, or point-of-view, as a communication;

whether regarding energy or its condensation as matter—
a particle or bit that must ebb and flow and therefore creates a wave-flow motion to exist. The distance between the
source-point and any other receipt-point defines "space";
and the interval of transmission, "time."

An Alpha Spirit may originate a communication for expression along the Zu-line into existence, but there is
already a significant amount of past communications, erroneously imprinted associations and incomplete cycles of
action still running on personal circuits. This type of fragmentation actually inhibits clear communication because
there is existing interference on the line. Even when it is
coherent enough to be relayed among them, most human
communication is **aberrative**.

> At the upper (*Alpha*) levels of the Standard Model:
>
> The Alpha Spirit (7.0) is a communication or wave-
> crest ridge on a Sea of Infinity (8);
>
> Alpha Thought (6.0) is a communication or wave-
> form projected from the Alpha Spirit (7.0) into the
> ALL of "Spiritual Existence" where the Self may
> postulate, theorize, create and form any images for
> consideration;
>
> Will-Intention (5.0) is a communication between
> the *Alpha* states and control systems for beta or ma-
> terial existence—or else, where the Spirit com-
> mands the Master Control Center (or MCC) for
> managing experience of beta-existence.

Goals for basic systemology include increasing defragmented channels for considerations—meaning free and uninhibited consideration and a willingness to communicate
any willed intention based on true judgment and not
based on the fragmentary images and emotional associations that may be heavily attached to these channels.

Full capability along any/all channels to any terminal would be simply the:

Willingness to send/transmit any communication;

Willingness to receive/accept any communication; and

Understand/Duplicate the communication free of turbulence/emotional charge.

In systematic processing of the "Willingness to Communicate" a Pilot is assisting the *Seeker* in overcoming inhibitions, reducing fragmentation, dispersing emotional charges and other erroneously imprinted beliefs and associations regarding the "Willingness to Communicate." Systematic processing may be applied to any facet of the human experience and beyond even that—but it seems relevant and appropriate to provide this one as a practical example here.

All basic processing presented in systemology is toward the increase of ability by increasing an individual's willingness *to be able*—and in essence, *be* responsible *for*. We treat the subject of responsibility as a separate class of processing, but that is not to say that a *Seeker* will not come to the appropriate realization that all "power" comes from the responsibility to be Self-directed as a creative force in existence. A *Seeker* may even come to the greater realization that all of their fragmentation is self-fed and unnecessarily reproduced in the mind.

:: 5 ::
TWO-WAY COMMUNICATION SYSTEMS

Communication puts a potential pathway into existence between two points—of which we may refer to as "viewpoints" (POV). Every point in space is a potential POV—which is an upper-level *realization* that results from processing. Our knowledge is a "systemology" because we may use it to apply a philosophy that is effective for all relative systems, not just specific instances. For example: the same "source-point to receipt-point" (or sender-receiver) circuit between a Pilot and *Seeker* in a session describes a cycle-of-action called the "communication circuit" which also demonstrates truths of communication between Alpha and Beta control points (or **anchor** points) of an Identity-Continuum.

Direction and flow of two-way communication in the piloted session is a responsibility of the Pilot. The Pilot must be in control of this flow in order to ensure proper processing. But, it should be understood that as an applied spiritual philosophy, Systemology is not some newfangled psychoanalysis mental health science concerned with talk therapies and associative free thought. Undirected communication cycles are a waste of time for both the Pilot and *Seeker*.

Systematic processing is a "selective direction of attention" and when engaged properly, the methodology does produce *actualized realizations* for a *Seeker*. But, the Pilot and *Seeker* must be both *fully present* and participating in the session to yield any benefits. This requires a very specific and controlled handling of communications. Communication and control are the keys to all effective systematic processing sessions.

Piloted Two-Way Communication is not a "conversation" in the traditional sense; certainly not as such that the *Seeker* might receive from their average friend or family member—or anywhere in the typical social environment of the standard-issue human condition.

Systematic Processing is not designed to directly treat conditions of a "body" or "genetic vehicle" with the exception of increasing personal "control *of*" a body *as* a vehicle. This conception is envisioned by some as "control of" a marionette doll—but under no circumstances should a Pilot validate entrapment of a Seeker *being* stuck "in" a "physical body."

The proper use of systematic processing and command lines should always direct a *Seeker's* attention to the control and monitoring of the body, rather than any identification of *Self* being forced "into" a body. Whenever a body is treated, the statements are always in relation to controlling the centers of "a" body or "that" body, but never enforcing a *Seeker's* considerations that *they are their physical body*. The sooner a *Seeker* can begin to treat the control and imagery of the body as though it is out "in front" of them, the better.

In the "systemology of universal physics" explored in *Grade-III*,[*] a *Seeker* discovers that the cosmos and entire Identity-continuum related to I-AM-*Self* is entirely composed of energetic interactions and communications taking place between the two cosmic principles: substance and motion. And of course when we add personal *Awareness* to the equation, we arrive at the various 'circuit-flows' able to be experienced as an *is*. As a 'motion', Zu is the energetic activity in the cosmos, exchange of information and interactive communications that vibrate within and also radiate flows from out all forms, which carry them through space as points measured in time.

> "Zu is not literally and exclusively the 'Mind'—which is a 'system' of manifestations that processes and otherwise <u>communicates</u> the Zu apparent as 'personal awareness'... A *Seeker's* own understanding—and the ability to share such 'Reality' with

---

[*]   Refer to *"The Tablets of Destiny"* and *"The Power of Zu."*

> others—will always rely on the <u>communication</u> of information and energy, both among one's own personal systems and in any interactions with other systems."   —The Power of Zu (Liber-S1Z)

Whenever a Pilot determines a *Seeker* has a source of turbulence on a particular channel or with a particular terminal, the most basic solution is to regain control of the communication with that aspect or terminal. Imprinting creates barriers to a full range of consideration and willingness, creating conditions that enforce specific programming or reactive-responses in place of true Self-determined thought activity. A Pilot must eventually be able to distinguish between true Alpha Thought and mechanistic automation ('automatic circuits') often substituting such.

Beta-existence is very much 'physical' and very much 'mechanistic'—having reached such a state of solidarity in particles and flows that at its most continuous level it can be seen to be arranged or 'cosmically ordered' as a series of 'clockwork' systems. The slippery slope or downward spiral begins with accepting consideration that all systems must be rigidly material and 'clockwork', thereby keeping the 'free range of thought' of the individual fixed into certain-or-specific modes along certain-and-specific channels with certain-and-specific terminals, &tc.

Two-way communication—as it relates to a piloted session —assists in determining if a *Seeker* is "in **phase**" and "present" (which addresses the "presence" factor of the session). Part of this step in the process includes establishing what, if any, current "problems and concerns" might be keeping attention on matters outside the session.

The purpose here is not to literally solve an individual's perceived problems one by one, but simply to make certain that they are acknowledged and then treated as not being present in the session. Whatever the specific nature of these, it is doubtful that any one of them is the actual source of fragmentation to be treated with systematic processing. It is much more likely that the chronic state of uncertainty an individual maintains is simply a contributor to their "handling" or "management" of problem-solving capabilities.

Using basic relays of communication at the beginning of the session assists directing a *Seeker's* attention to the session itself. For example: asking a *Seeker* if there is anything you should know about, or if there is anything going on in their life right now that might put focus out of session. An interest in the *Seeker* and their management of living conditions outside of the sessions also assists in establishing greater trust in the Pilot by the *Seeker*. It should also be evident, though not necessarily stated directly, that assistance is available and the Pilot is there to help them.

Communication is Will-Intention *in action*. It is the intent to cause an effect; even if that effect is simply duplication of some message or energy. We have established that the effective quality of the communication is proportional or equivalent to the duplication (perception, understanding and interpretation) "A-for-A." The "sender" of a communication acts as the primary 'cause' for that cycle, and the "receiver" must be willing to accept the communication flow as an 'effect' in order for there to be duplication or reproduction of the intention as effect.

Previously, "communication lag" is described as distortions in circuitry that fragment a "communication line." This fragmentation is noticeable during systematic processing or when an individual is communicating their considerations. Rather than acting from an *Alpha* point of Will (&tc.), the individual's *Actualized Awareness* is heavily charged and engulfed in a lot of "sticky-like" beliefs, postulates, personal creations and agreements with others that filter a communication with the environment where Awareness is fixed. As we know, the greater the distance, even on something as abstract as the "Zu-line" on the Standard Model, the greater the probability of fragmentation and distortion; and the longer its communication lag.

The immediacy and "presence" found in being centered in the "Now" (or the "kNow" as we used to write it a decade ago in the original systemology thesis papers) is of such importance, that without this prerequisite state, no actual "session" has begun. Once a session has begun, a Pilot must make certain that each cycle of communication in the session is completed before originating another.

The basic wave-arc or cycle-of-action for two-way communication is:

— a) an origination at the source-point

→ b) reception at receipt-point and response

→ c) response is acknowledged by original source-point

→ d) receipt-point knows the cycle has been completed

| All systematic processing requires
completing the cycle of action for each command line. |

The command line is an "input" into a system. The communication line is a "flow of information" and a "circuit" is formed when there are "two-way comm-lines" established between two "terminals." All masses and "resistances" create fragmentation, ridges and jagged flows. This all sounds rather technical; though in practice, the demonstrations show that the technicality of our vocabulary is simply best for the widest range of systematic application.

We discovered that one of the reasons "Self-Processing"∞ has limitations, is that even just the continuous use of autosuggestion or auto-commands concerning recall or other directions has a tendency to set up new "circuits" in the mind to relay this type of third-person communication to *Self*.*

The creation of any point or consideration or thought or energy stream requires an equal creation of appropriated space for it to exist—which is to say a "field" by which the

---

∞ Self-processing, refer to *Crystal Clear (Liber-2B)*.

* Solo-Piloting (or Solo-Flying) is instructed at higher *Grades*.

encoding and decoding of a message can take place between two terminals. This "field" or "zone" is also known as the area of potential interference, because it exists in a space between the sender and receiver. The space will carry the message clearly in the absence of interference.

Another source of interference is the "personal circuit"—which is to say the processing (of Zu) taking place interior to the Personal Identity Continuum of an individual. Yes, the individual is a terminal, but they are more than just a solid wall (we would hope anyways; it's possible that they *are* that apathetic) and therefore have an entire systematic process taking place within the domain of their own personal beta (internal) or alpha (exterior spiritual) experience.

A "personal circuit" can also become fragmented when an individual sets up additional internalized communication circuits with terminals that have been imagined into beingness and used as a substitute to discharge communication flows against. If an individual does not feel or perceive any response from a communication line, a sort of self-made mechanism of automatic response will be generated to maintain a continuous energy action on that terminal—even outside the conscious awareness and Will of the individual that first set it up!

The more an energy flow is generated toward mental images on an automatic loop and seemingly without *Self-direction*, the more that these imprinted "facsimiles" or "copies" of reality will seem more and more solid; treated more and more like the "real thing" when the control of these automatic response mechanisms is no longer treated as the responsibility of the *Self*.

A response by the *Seeker* to the 'processing command line' is not the end of a communication cycle. Doing so would keep the attention flow on the *Seeker* as an effect only—which is simply one step toward poorly handled interrogation. The *Seeker* remains an effect-point until they (their answer/response) is acknowledged. Acknowledgment is acknowledgment; the *Seeker's* response only needs to be acknowledged as extant in order to complete the current cycle. For example: the delivery of the same command line a second (or third...&tc.) time is not a repeat of the same communication; each is its own cycle—its own space and time. Proper management of communication of energy is what control of true power *is*!

A fragmented Alpha Spirit left to its own devices has already traversed uppermost **echelons** of spiritual existences and various universes as reality—but the true underlying nature of existence can become quite empty and forbidding when the Spirit projects its Awareness to points in this newly perceived space and then finds nothing in the environment answering communications. This is the nature of Alpha fragmentation: a Spirit waits longer and longer for a response and becomes more and more fixated on the spaces and "things" as a result. Differentiating energies (material solids from living forms) is resolved during "communication processing."

The Pilot and *Seeker* are both treated (rightfully) as "live terminals" during the "session." They are not the only "terminals" extant; but for purposes of *Professional Piloting Procedure*, they are the only "live terminals" with a "presence" in the "session."

Objective processing also produces great results on the *Pathway to Self-Honesty* prior to pushing a *Seeker* through a series of intensive mental exercises. It is suggested to alternate subjective and objective processing during a session. Pilots use objective processing to assist getting the *Seeker's* focus and command of the body under their own Self-control. This provides an ability to grant "presence"

as *Self* within the session. Entangled energy may even be discharged on solid forms (physical terminals) in the physical universe, which do not otherwise act as living terminals—such as inert matter, objects and walls. Hence, the incorporation of 'objective processing' which can assist in both grounding or centering the *Seeker* in good communication with the physical universe and also helping to consciously knowingly maintain their own perspective or "viewpoint" (POV) on reality "in phase" with the "*present.*"

Pilots assist a *Seeker* in establishing communication lines (or flows) with the appropriate terminals so that a seeker may discharge their own fragmented stores of energy on another terminal (other than the Pilot) and 'ground out' the energetic charge. The Pilot is of course educated to understand and maintain full knowledge of the types of phenomenon or manifestations that may potentially present themselves while processing a *Seeker*, including intensive emotional discharges and/or other "loop patterns" expressed.

Piloted sessions are effective when a *Seeker* is successfully directed to access their own programming and emotional encoding, imprinting and fragmentation, when facets that would otherwise be unknowingly restimulative are not actively present in the environment. This gives a *Seeker* the chance *to see* a facet, bit of data or mental image for what it *is* in Self-Honesty—and "**process out**" stores of reactive-response charges along the way.

Basic establishment of a "session" and the communication cycle-of-action that follows as "processing" is easily summarized in four fundamental steps:

A.) The Pilot (*sender*) sees that the Seeker (*receiver*) is in session, prepared to be a receipt-point for communication;

B.) The Pilot (*sender*) selects a communication channel or line and directs a query or transmission to the Seeker (*receiver*);

C.) The Pilot (*sender*) sees that the transmission is received by the Seeker (*receiver*); and

—a secondary cycle-of-action ensues while the Seeker performs a personal communication on their own circuits after processing it; and

—the resulting response to the query or processing line is communicated from the Seeker (now a *sender*) back to the Pilot (now a *receiver*).

D.) The Pilot then acknowledges receipt and comprehension of the communications to complete the cycle.

Any breakdown in this flow (cycle-of-action just described) must be addressed immediately during the session in order to maintain an effective session and before attempting to resolve or complete additional cycles (commands, processing, &tc). Remember that it is the Pilot's responsibility to ensure this flow takes place as described; so, we will examine each of the parts a little closer before moving on.

A.) The Pilot (*sender*) sees that the Seeker (*receiver*) is in session, prepared to be a receipt-point for communication;

Before any actual systematic processing begins, the "presence" of both the Pilot and the Seeker must be established; and subsequently prior to the transmission of each cycle of communication. Of course, once a session is running well, it may take but a moment to be sure that the Seeker is ready for the next command line. Although technically some kind of "processing" begins as soon as the Seeker has walked in through the door to the session environment, an actual "session" has not really begun until "presence" has been established.

There are many ways in which "presence" may not be able to be present, therefore preventing a proper session from actually starting. These may include any personal issues that the Seeker is experiencing regarding the location of the session, the individual acting as the Pilot or any other pressing concerns affecting the mind from outside the environment.

Once these preliminaries have been addressed, the next major concern of the Pilot is making sure that the Seeker is able to "duplicate communications"—that a willing Alpha Spirit is able to maintain enough control over functions of the physical body in order to actual be receipt-point, receive transmissions properly, comprehend them and process them internally—all of which is implied when we define these qualities at once as a "duplication."

These are many gradient levels of response to systematic processing; including the entire band of potential "experience"—from the lowest range of near-body-death up to the moment when a being now actualized with the full state of *Awareness* as the I-AM-Self would be able to generate an entirely new universe for itself whilst standing at its own Alpha state of existence as a wave ridge or peak amidst a sea of Infinity. Unnecessary stresses on the Seeker (and a Pilot straining to be successful) are avoided by not making the Seeker confront a larger gradient or higher tier of actualization than they have achieved a realization for. An individual is only capable of being *Aware* and willing and determined to the extent that they have established for themselves. This must be increased at a pace that is effectively appropriate.

B.) The Pilot (*sender*) selects a communication channel or line and directs a query or transmission to the Seeker (*receiver*);

The Pilot is trained to direct the Seeker's attentions with communication; therefore if these skills have not been reached, there is more likelihood for a breakdown in the cycle. Processing is dependent on the ability of the Pilot to maintain and hold the Seeker's attention for the duration of the session. "Interest" levels lie within the band of "thought" and not "emotion"—meaning that interest is not manged by the RCC (reactive-response) system, but requires that this system not be engaged or restimulated so that a Seeker may be *Self-directed* in their focus of attention. If the Pilot pushes the Seeker into too steep of a gradient in processing, the Seeker will find themselves confused and "stalling out" in interest (which may trigger reactive-responses). Maintaining control of the communication and command lines is the Pilot's responsibility.

C.) The Seeker receives the communication, duplicates the data and processes it. Communication of the result is returned to (sent back to) the Pilot. The return communication is a performance of the process (such as an answer), or an indication (announcement) that a creative command line has been run.

Pilots encourage continuous flow of communication during the session, including to notice when a Seeker is getting hung up. Keep in mind that we are dealing with an active flow between living terminals of a system, so a Seeker should be encouraged with gentle prompts to continue any flow they are processing; but also making sure that the Seeker is not lost in their own circuitry. We can assume that Seekers have already spent too much of their lifetime (or several lifetimes) internalizing with various circuits or running around the physical universe trying to communicate with dead terminals. Systematic processing is meant to remedy this condition.

D.) The Pilot then acknowledges receipt and comprehension of the communications to complete the cycle.

In order to complete (close) one cycle of the communication circuit, the Pilot is required to acknowledge the communication flow of the Seeker. Failure to do so is one of the most invalidating aspects of the communication process; and this truth is not exclusively limited to applications of *Professional Piloting Procedure*, but in all aspects of Life and the Universe.

An acknowledgment within the session assists the *Seeker* in their certainty to realize greater flows of attention (*Awareness*) are placed onto the circuits processed in the session than would otherwise be the case if the *Seeker* were left alone to their own resolve—either to Self-Process or to be allowed to bump against all of the perceived blockages encountered in their environment as a radiated explosion of unfocused uncontrolled volatile chaotic energy.

Remember not to introduce a new communication/command cycle until the existing circuit has been either completed or repaired. It is better if no need to repair is present; hence we establish the most ideal practices for a Systemology Pilot (Air Command Pilots and Ministers of Mardukite Zuism, &tc.) that may be applied to any and all systematic processing session regardless of their level.

The Pilot therefore accepts any and all answers with an acknowledgment before proceeding to another, even if the earlier command line is to be used again. Even if the message is being repeated, it is for a new "prompt of an answer" and a new communication cycle.

Often the methods of systematic processing require the use of the same "command line" numerous times in order to breakthrough to the level of answers that will provide true realizations. This is not really the same command repeated many times, but each is its own command, with its own space-time.

A Pilot should never ask a Seeker to repeat their answer as if it were wrong—or to press the Seeker in any way as to whether or not *that* is actually their answer or if they actually performed the creative (subjective or mental image) command, &tc.

The answer *is* the answer; it is at least the Seeker's answer for that moment or instance of space-time. It is the answer for that moment of consideration toward the definition or implication of what a command means. But, as systematic processing undoubtedly demonstrates, the significances and meanings ascribed to things are purely circumstantial and entirely self-created. An individual has an ability to change these considerations at will—and as a result, has the ability to change how they are going to interact with any flow-line with any terminal in existence.

:: 6 ::
UNIVERSAL COMMUNICATION AS
A SYSTEMATIC CONTROL ACTION

Communication is a primary requirement for existence. There is a communication of *Spiritual Life Energy* ("ZU") present directly at each of the principles of manifestation: substance, motion and *Awareness*. Circulatory communication of Zu is present within and as each/all level/aspect of existence and manifestation. Everything alive is a communication. This activity within a Mind-System is the communication with the ZU/Awareness of a specific 'Personal Identity Continuum' that extends between an Alpha Spirit and a beta form.

Mardukite Systemology is derived from only one single assumption or primary postulate for which we have an understanding of Life, the Universe and Everything simply by further logical deduction and practical experiential experimentation directly in said universe by said Life to determine anything and about everything. (This is otherwise called *"epistemology."*)

The original premise is this: that the true *Self* or actual identity of the individual is an Alpha Spirit. This spirit is capable of the highest creativeness and is itself set in a high state of beingness, which later became the effect of its own creations: considerations, beliefs, imprinted associative knowledge, fragmented experience and over-identification with fixed states of beingness other than the *Self* as Alpha Spirit—which means, usually, an over-identification with the genetic vehicle (physical body) as the *Self*, and a belief that there is some way able to permanently hinder or harm the *Self* beyond or exterior to this beta existence. It is a primary purpose of systematic processing to return a Seeker the certainty of this state.

For all of its technical speech, *NexGen Systemology* is not a superficial presentation of *Life, the Universe and Everything*, such as we actually tend to find more within the lesser-level domains of physical knowledge and even conventional metaphysics. Our entire field is based on only one grand assumption—one main tenet that cannot necessarily be directly proven within the confines of *beta-existence*, and that is:

YOU, the actual *I-AM-Self*, is an Alpha Spirit.

This is all that an individual is required to "take on faith" until it may be known—and since we are dealing with the "spiritual" in these matters, there are many who simply find the validity of *Mardukite Systemology* as an extension of one of the oldest religious and mystical orders to develop from the Ancient Mystery School, called *Mardukite Zuism* for our purposes. There are many schools of thought that are based on opposite assumptions, and these tend to be more in line with what an individual is typically indoctrinated to believe. There are many esotericists, elitists, philosophers and other intellectual authorities, which believe (or enforce the belief) that "common man, the animal" (the standard-issue human condition) is not capable of actualizing any greater state of beingness—or that only a select demographic of the population is somehow capable. We have not actually found any workable truth to these statements.

A more effective truth, which may be demonstrated with systematic processing, is that while not entering the "Great Work" on the same level, *all humans* have the innate ability to reclaim and reawaken the knowing embedded deep within as the power of the Spirit. Just as an individual's *Awareness* (sense of Self) can be fixed to lower-points of beingness by selective direction of attention, so can it be "unfixed." In doing so, and being free to consider its more natural Alpha States, it finds that far more than an "identifying" with a particular body or set of life-memory and emotional mechanisms, the Alpha state is a beingness equivalent to the other alpha states it gives consideration to—which means the actual true I-AM-Self *is*

Spirit, *is* Alpha Thought, and *is* Will. This is just as comparable to the beta-experience of a "Mind-Body" that carries
thoughts and emotions and applies effort, though these
are treated at a lower-order of existence, being confined
entirely to the "beta"/physical universe.

Levels of *Awareness* correspond to communications exchanged by an individual—which is of course more significantly noticeable in family units and social organizations. Fragmentation becomes most obvious within gener-
alization. We also see the chronic beta-state of *Awareness*
manifest in the very types of communication that an individual is *willing* to pass along; or how they filter or alter a
message to meet their level of understanding and emotional condition.

You can look at any point on the *Beta-Awareness Scales* (and
the simplified   *Emotimeter* scale) and identify individuals
in your life (or perhaps in your past) that only seem to
communicate after engaging one of those lower-level reactive-response mechanisms for the processing: an individual, for example, that only communicates bad news; or
another that only communicates antagonistic gossip; or
another that insistently invalidates others with only coun-
ter-points, and so forth.

As memory gathers mass, other people attach certain
"personality" stereotypes to individuals carrying chronic
states. These observations become basis for additional
judgments and considerations that further enter the equation. This is simply another example of why all interpersonal communication outside of a state of Self-Honesty is
highly *aberrative* and leads to personal fragmentation.

In our modern "electronic-age"-meets-"space-age" society, we are most likely to best understand the concepts of
"terminals" in relation to how we tend to socially use the
"term" today: as a mass that is able to communicate data,
process commands—essentially any of the input–output
functions that we should expect—such as in the case of a
"computer terminal" which may also "interface" or com-

municate with *other* "terminals." When we chart out "network systematics," these terminals are also treated as "nodes."

> terminal (node) : a point, end or mass on a line; a point or connection for closing an electric circuit, such as a post on a battery terminating at each end of its own systematic function; any end point or 'termination' on a line; a point of connectivity with other points; in systems, any point which may be treated as a contact point of interaction; anything that may be distinguished as an 'is' and is therefore a 'termination point' of a system or along a flow-line which may interact with other related systems it shares a line with; a point of interaction with other points.

To provide another application, let us take up the example of "Systemology" as a "terminal." It is an *is*—meaning it *is* some *thing* which may be ascribed data, associations and significances. You can read a book about it. You can talk about it with friends. You can form an opinion about it if your experience with it suddenly becomes imprinted by some or another emotional charge, and so on.

As an *abstract* concept, "Systemology" would not be considered a "living terminal"; it is not a specific individuated lifeforce-entity which will communicate with you. But that does not mean it is not a *real* terminal—it is simply not a *concrete* one. That later quality is something which individuals actual cause by concentrating more and more mass on the terminal. But so long as it may be brought to an individual's level of *reality* in some way, it will be *real* to the extent that a person can hold a circuit of reality on it.

For example, if you take up communicating about Systemology to another individual, most will usually respond positively unless it is somehow already associated with some imprint that has a heavy emotional charge that the individual takes as negative. An example of this is would be someone that associates the individual, unique, specific idea of Systemology with something else—for example, an "alien cult." A person reads the word "Anunnaki" on a title of a book by Joshua Free, watches a television program by a completely different author, then sees something about "processing fragmentation of the human condition" and finally reads a website about a sci-fi alien cult in California that committed suicide. They then start to group these different terminals along the same line and suddenly decide that this method of Self-Help is actually an alien cult... *False logic.*

We cannot dismiss the very fact that this is how the human condition learns and associates its knowledge. The Mind-System is an incredible tool for interaction with the physical universe, but its certainty of calculation is always 100% no matter how valid the inputs really are. When an individual does not have any "reality" on some terminal, they do not share communication with it; they aren't going to "like" it—thereby will not want it "close" to them in proximity. They are not going to be "interested" in it—and are likely to dismiss it with a response of "boredom." All of this is due to numerous past failures to understand something new, which after accumulating, will inhibit an individual's willingness to "reach" toward a terminal to understand it or bring it "closer." How an individual might treat an object (terminal) in space is no different than their handling of mental images treated as "things."

We notice certain tendencies with those that have self-made or agreed-upon deficiencies in learning new things—mostly stemming from emotional encoding on the circuits connected to education, studying, learning, schoolwork, new databanks (books), and other such inputs. Some individuals have had "such a bad go" at these terminals in the past that they now have become entirely convinced there is something wrong with them. This can happen with any "terminal" in existence; we are simply using "learning" as an example. New materials (books) or new information are intended to lead to new considerations. First among these are the **semantics** (or syntax) connected to the vocabulary and terminology used to define the paradigm. This is important for understanding the rest.

Once the arrangement of semantics has been grouped and organized as a preliminary level of understanding, later incorporation of new data within that paradigm or field of study is then "learned" based on definitions of the vocabulary in relation to demonstrations made that are then compared as similar or dissimilar to what an individual already knows (has established as fact cumulatively up to that point). As an increased understanding is maintained, more focused attention may be given to the subject—and the increased familiarity will result in an increased liking, acceptance or agreement concerning that subject/terminal, and therefore a greater willingness to "reach" toward and bring into closer proximity and thus responsibility of communication.

Something that is found effective toward positive results is likely to be of interest; and the increase of true understanding in Self-Honesty is most certainly a very positive result and a reassurance for effectiveness. A person is likely to repeat or follow or keep close that which *works* and is *effective* in *producing positive results*. For what other basis do we have for anything?

Control and communication operate systematically to create considerations of space-time:

COMMUNICATION—the idea, thought, concept, wave-action, bit or particle that is in motion creating the space about it.

CONTROL—the direction/directed intent that drives focus or attention of the idea, thought, concept, wave-action, bit or particle as a communication.

SPACE—the energy/mass created as a result of communication and control.

The *Grade-III* Textbooks/Self-Help Manuals—*Tablets of Destiny* and *Crystal Clear*—are combined to help resolve some of the most basic issues facing operators of the human condition, which correspond with increasing personal management beyond the common level of standard-issue programming and fragmentation-producing social involvement. Using the material given in the previous Grade, it is expected that a *Seeker* or *Pilot-in-Training* has:

a) accrued a basic education in the terminology and basic theory of Systemology;

b) ability to effective apply the basic tech to personal life and yield results;

c) attained a certainty that their personal situation will not get any worse;

d) increased determination to self-process and receive professional processing toward greater improvement of Self-Actualization;

e) ability to achieve higher actualized Awareness and knowing to manage most affairs of physical existence with certainty and as cause, overcoming worries and false hopes;

f) the actualized ability to "self-help" (literally) and the realization that we must use our abilities to help others— *all* Life in Existence...

...which naturally brings us to *Grade-IV* and the basic tools inherently necessary for such ventures—being the emphasis, of course, of the current textbook of Piloting Procedure.

Communication is a direction of control, which is of course most applicable to the personal identity continuum and its control of a body in the physical universe. The communication that makes this systematically possible actually originates from outside of, or exterior to, the *beta-existence* (physical universe) itself. It is quite simply a sheer act of Will, and therefore the highest facet of beta-control that *Self* has at its disposal. Everything that the *Self* is *doing* is a communication out into universes—at least two: a personal spiritual universe (*Alpha*) and a physical universe (*beta*). Alpha Communication is a creative expression of the Alpha Spirit as I-AM-Self. Self generates an Alpha Thought as manifestation—and this creation is controlled by Will-intention at the upper-levels of Alpha or Spiritual existence, exterior to a physical body and even the Mind-Systems that connects the Alpha Spirit as an identity along the *continuum* of energetic control centers that make *beta-existence* with a *genetic vehicle* even possible.

The nature of Intention and the activities of the Will are the closest points from the Alpha spectrum to the Beta spectrum (of the Zu-line on the Standard Model). On the beta side, the uppermost reach is the "Mind-System" itself. The Mind-System is an intermediary between what is taking place as Will-Intention (Alpha) and what information is directed toward the control of a physical body. But these flows are not one-way. They also send information back to Self, which constitutes any further considerations or analysis or estimations.

When the channels are not cleared, but are instead filled with debris and fragmentation, the information and energy that is communicate along the lines in each direction will be filtered or altered by some other type of imprinted or encoded influence—and thus we say that the information, the experience of the information and any further considerations of significance assigned to the information is all "fragmented."

As a Seeker resurfaces their associations on any given channel (circuit with a terminal), data may be brought to a scrutiny at analytical levels based on a specific "point-of-view" (POV). Each consideration has the ability to change the way in which the channel is treated until the Seeker is actualizing a realization that they have the ability to change this POV at Will.

Each terminal node is a potential point of contact and it is that "contact of a terminal" that the Pilot is most concerned with in directed the focused attention of a Seeker. An individual has the ability to "contact" points of energy and matter in space and across time (as recorded on their personal timeline)—and this includes the points on the timeline when we have fixed those considerations, imprints and beliefs in place, even if we have since forgotten that they are there. The point is to remember that they are there, so they may be brought to a scrutiny analytically as a consideration the individual is free to create anew —but how would this be possible if the individual did not realize they had put the first point out there as a "solid" in the first place? Otherwise the original creation would go on continuing perpetually to exist outside of the responsibility and control of its creator.

Accumulation of "experience" seems to create more barriers to communication and willingness than it resolves; yet humans tend to very much value "experience" above the achievement of an ideal state of Knowing and Being, even when such begins to define or restrict the individual to smaller more rigid parameters of what is real or possible.

A Pilot uses systematic processing to assist the Seeker in widening the consideration of their "viewpoints" (POV)— which in turn allows for a natural increase in actualized personal realizations without educational indoctrination toward a specific result or concept. It is simply a matter of allowing the Seeker the freedom of ability to manage the mental images and their associations that have all been collected, quite simply, by what a Seeker has been exposed to.

Inflows and outflows of energy are exchanged in a circuit. A completed circuit allows a flow of energy. An imbalance in flow direction alone is enough to cause turbulence on that channel and increases likelihood of imprinted fragmentation. You can easily notice in a conversation how an individual that is projecting a communication will become frustrated when they are not receiving back any kind of answer or response. And those which are in the habit of only accepting inflows of communication equally become frustrated when they are not given a chance to originate their own communications. One of the most important steps for good communication, managing personal life, managing abilities of the spirit and conducting the most effective optimum piloting is capability and willingness to *confront*.

> confront : to come around in front of; to be in the presence of; to stand in front of, or in the face of; to meet "face-to-face" or "face-up-to."

Many individuals may have a fragmented understanding of the concept of "confronting" due to its improper handling and associative "experiential knowledge." There are some that have come to "opinion" that all *confrontation* is "bad." Apparently they have the concept of confronting confused with semantics of *conflict*, or opposition to "good communication." And then there are those which seem to have mastered no other levels of communication but to be in conflict with everything in their environment and seek to impose or enforce any and all manner of arbitraries onto it in lacking for true control.

An ability to hold attention and control of the session; the ability to deliver communications as though they are your own even when read from a book or list; the ability to ensure complete communication cycles during processing; these are responsibilities of the Pilot—and additionally to be able to conduct this activity without becoming fragmented by the Seeker or the operations of the session. All of this may be resolved with proper practice of communication skills, the ability to confront/interface properly with a Seeker (or any individual that you maintain a presence with), the ability to deliver communications, then acknowledge receipt of a response to those communications and expertly bridge them to the next cycle of communications.

Individuals who are able to direct their attention with fixed focus and concentration easily are able to also manage their own internalized communications and handle their own reactive "Self-talk" and "out of phase" assumptions taken on from others with greater ease—if these types of reactive-response mechanisms are still functioning at all. The ability to be at ease and comfortable "in the face" of other individuals and terminals is one of the indicators of Self-Honesty—and what we mean by the ability to confront.

Those who are more *Self-directed* and operate more clearly from the Alpha states of Will and Intention are also able to better focus their own energies and direct their own attention as needed without becoming either unnecessarily fixed or distracted, but under the full control of Self. The greater certainty an individual maintains that they are able to handle a situation or terminal, the more willing they are to face it. Often this must be practiced or worked up to on a gradient scale, but it is possible to achieve states whereby an individual is willing to confront and manage anything that "life" can throw... and still walk away smiling.

> "We should not be surprised that behaviors and realities—activities and motions—manifested in the Physical Universe from individuals 'blocked' or 'fragmented' by many imposed artificial solids are also blocking others in their energy flow. These are often the same individuals that seek incessant validation of their own 'fragmentation' by forcefully trying to 'make us as they are.' It is only when we return to our true sense of Self that we are stronger as individuals—with a higher frequency of operation—in our ability to <u>confront</u> energy and transform obstacles to our survival in the Physical Universe as daily life, and free our Self to experience its highest spiritual evolution and Awareness as 'I AM.'"   —The Tablets of Destiny (Liber-One)

> "Aside from those memories assumed through direct 'bodily injury,' disruptive Imprints are mainly a result of authoritarian enforcement of beliefs, 'emotional baggage' and other programmed responses that strongly influence our thought fragmentation from beneath an emotional surface—and which is prone to resurface unbidden and undirected by the Self. These types of Imprints must be

systematically 'resurfaced' and '_confronted_' on the _Pathway to Self-Honesty_ before effectively defragmenting 'higher energy' thought-bases of manifestation: substance, motion and Awareness—of which these Imprints will undoubtedly distort in the Mind. Remember that we cannot move forward past the point we do not understand—and this very much includes ourselves and our relationship ties to the past."   — Tablets of Destiny (Liber-One)

"When we are able to Self-Honestly resurface and _confront_ the ridiculousness of our past—'look back and laugh'—we are immediately released from the emotional hold that it has on us. We have brought it all up to the surface for the Mind-Systems to deal with appropriately by Self-direction and we reduce the automated programming that is attached to it."
                —The Tablets of Destiny (Liber-One)

"Too often, this idea of 'positive thinking' or 'creative visualization' or a few minutes spent in front of the mirror chanting 'axioms' and 'affirmations' is not enough to override lifetimes of bombardment— or even the interference prevalent in a single lifetime in the 'modern' world. The Human Condition requires a bit more assistance now to grant the certainty necessary to rise up and _confront_ the sources of turbulence—thereby preventing further and additional fragmentation."   —The Power of Zu

As a Pilot: the ability to confront or face the Seeker is the first step to having any flow of communication for a session. This means the ability to _be_ and share a _presence_ with the Seeker. Just as it is important to get a Seeker to be focused and attentive to the session with their presence, so too must the Pilot be fully present for the session—and fully able to face the Seeker with actualized Awareness.

A Pilot practices facing turbulence with ease; or at least the demonstration to all concerned that it is being handled with ease. Even when the "plane is going down," the Pilot must be expert at maintaining their own composure to ensure that they can control the communication of energy taking place in their environment and thereby provide greater certainty or stability to the composure of the passengers. It may be assumed that a Pilot will encounter an entire array of potential phenomenon and manifestations from Seekers as they handle the processing sessions—and it is the responsibility of the Pilot to simply maintain the integrity of the session in every instance.

A Pilot practices using communications and processes alone, using basic objective processing* or even a "stuffed animal." It is better if they are able to be coached by someone that can observe them; particularly in exercises that are meant as training for "living communication" between beings. The purpose is to practice "not reacting" to whatever the other person is doing or saying. Before even introducing other steps, such as delivering a communication or acknowledgment, a Pilot should begin by practicing simply *being* in the *presence* of another without flinching or apologizing or performing any unnecessary (and often unintentional) body movement, coughing, fidgeting &tc.

A person might start by just getting used to being in the spatial vicinity of some terminal, and therefore not even look; just sitting a few feet across from another person even when you are not looking at them will still require you to *be* in their *presence*. You can try practicing with eyes closed and then when that is comfortable, with eyes open; simply being in the presence of another for several minutes and able to do so comfortably. This may be practiced rigorously as needed. It is a valuable skill. It does not denote any type of agreement or status with what is being confronted, but simply the ability to face it and not quiver away from it or evade it or react to it out of discomfort with small smirks and giggles, noticeably widening eyes or even verbal responses and interjections that are not spec-

---

*   Refer to *"Crystal Clear"* or Grade-III *"Systemology Handbook."*

ifically part of the process.

The most important thing to understand about the ability to confront, if nothing else, is that it is a state of *beingness;* it is not something you are doing. True ability to confront as Self does not require any other automatic mechanisms or social conventions, such as those that we might inherently begin to assume for ourselves after repeated experiences with the company of others. There are certain tendencies that often get set up based on these experiences and then used toward the handling of future experiences, nearly automatically. In other words, many have lost the ability to *confront and be* without *doing* something, particularly with regard to the body. This is one more consideration that an individual has made and agreed to at some point, which actually keeps them snapped harder *into* a body with beliefs that they are not to be able to confront anything of any universe without the body.

Technically, communication *is* the *Self-direction* of *intention.* An individual is *intending* something when they originate a communication or creation of any kind. This includes a written command line or some other piece of communication from another source. It must be owned and understood to be communicated. Due to the nature of individualism, creativity and the actualization of Will-Intention needed to engage a true communication, it is no wonder that so many individuals have dropped off their pathway with this step; whether approaching it as we currently describe, or even in the manner of which these very same type of preliminaries are found in many esoteric schools and philosopho-mystical traditions. For example, the purpose of any "ritual" is to *Self-direct* intention, and yet most practitioners will tend to get caught up in intricacies of the "ritual." As soon as considerations of ability become fixed to only having such and such power and ability during such and such times and by the authority of such and such of the umteenth legion of the second order of angelic hordes...well, then they have missed the whole point of "magic."

As with many other very critical preliminaries of both our "applied systemology" of the future and "applied magic and mysticism" of yesteryear, the significance, for example, of properly directing Will and Intention is so overlooked and yet is essentially the definition of what the individual has set out to do in the first place. If your current tradition, practices and techniques are not moving you along the Pathway in the direction of an increased certainty and willingness to direct intention, then you may want to rethink your approach. The purpose of practicing a controlled delivery of intended communication is so that the Pilot has the certainty and command to direct very clear intention as a message or direction of attention and *know* that this intention is being received and effects (duplicated) properly.

:: 7 ::
UNIVERSAL COMMUNICATION, WILL
AND THE POWER OF INTENTION

Intention generates energy behind communication—not the words. Of course there are many associations with words, starting with definitions we ascribe to them—and yet in true communication, intention is superior to words. The stronger the intention, the more likely it is to push through filters and fragmentation, but that does not mean that the intention itself is any clearer. Clarity is also subject to the debris, imprinting and filters on the communication line or channel—and any meaning assigned to symbols, words, &tc.

The Communication is the Intention (Alpha) on a line; the Words are a Medium or Catalyst of the flow.

In fact, sometimes if your intention is strong and clear enough, it will be received even if the words are not ideal. But it is directed and focused toward a receipt-point or spot in space; whether or not we have identified that spot as occupied by an individual. In objective processing, this may be practiced as simply as saying "hello" to an "object," but more than simply using the words, actually practicing the intention that the message is to be carried to the receipt-point.

Another version of this exercise would have you practice projecting the same intention previously used out loud, but communicating it silently and projecting it into the center of the object. You could extend this exercise by changing a consideration that some other (nonsensical) word actually *means* "hello"—and then applying that word with the same intention, first as a spoken method and then silent. The real point is to practice the direction of Will as communication. This is not a general **elocution** course we are presenting here.

When we speak of intention, we literally mean Will-Intention (5.0) on the Standard Model and it is an alpha quality of existence; you will not actually find it directly within the Physical Universe, nor in the Mind-System that is connected to a body. The act of intending comes from *Self* and is practically a creative opposite condition to being reactive.

> <u>intention</u> : the directed application of Will; to intend (have "in Mind") or signify (give "significance" to) for or toward a particular purpose; in *NexGen Systemology* (from the *Standard Model*)—the spiritual activity at WILL (5.0) directed by an *Alpha Spirit* (7.0); the application of WILL as "Cause" from a higher order of Alpha Thought and consideration (6.0), which then may continue to relay communications as an "effect" in the universe.

As harmonics of the Standard Model suggest, the alpha quality of Will-Intention at (5.0) is the higher-dimensional equivalent along the personal identity continuum as we would find "Effort" (1.0) in the Physical Universe. At (5.0), the Alpha spirit is impressing the most condensed part of spiritual beingness into its environment—strong enough to impinge or influence the physical universe, using the Mind-System at (4.0). At (1.0) the physical body or genetic vehicle is engaging its most condensed part of physical beingness as a physical effort into the environment—strong enough to produce an effect at that level that it will be inertly balanced by the continuity of energy and matter in the Physical Universe (0.0).

> "Of the many ways in which beta-existence may diminish willingness (and capability) to Self-direct with certainty, the most critical fragmentation consistently received from others—and social environment—may be reduced to two main categories:
>
> a.) **Invalidation**; and b.) **Enforcement**.

Both methods involve strong emotionally charged communication of <u>intention</u>, effort and belief—and both 'wave-forms' of energy operate outside of Self-Honesty as a 'fallacy' purely for the fact that they come from (allegedly) 'authoritarian' sources. Any 'appeal to authority' in logic is a 'fallacy' and therefore fragmentation by definition."

—Crystal Clear (Liber-2B)

"'Imagination' and 'Individuality' are properties of the Alpha Spirit that exceed the boundaries of the Physical Universe. They may certainly be realized in the Physical Universe, but the 'ideas' begin or have a cause that is exterior to the Physical Universe—the parts used to express a unique individual creation are not just duplicating an existing archetype. We aren't talking about conceiving a 'better table' or something. We all know what a 'table' is. But that idea was first formed exterior to the Physical Universe and then realized into beta-existence by an <u>intention</u> of Will. They aren't just growing ready-built tables on trees or mining them out of the ground."   —Crystal Clear (Liber-2B)

"Each and every one of us has the ability to both **incite** or dissolve 'creation' with our Attention— our focused application of Self-directed Awareness. We may do this many times a day: we form an <u>intention</u> in our mind, create an entire 'mental image' and then erase it. This is the innate ability of Self to 'imagine.'"   —Crystal Clear (Liber-2B)

"Emotional energy can be created by WILL (<u>Intention</u>) without succumbing to the actual low-level emotional fragmentation in-and-of itself. As cause, WILL intends effect. It does not require exciting a personal display of emotion to accomplish this either—it may be accomplished solely due to <u>Alpha-Intention</u>. This is precisely how the 'I AM' as Alpha Spirit directs all cause and consciousness activity form the 'ACC' (7.0). Everything above (4.0) on the Standard Model and ZU-line (and any Systemology model, chart or scale) is considered 'causal' in terms of beta-existence. Using the power of Intention, the Seeker can simply 'Will' a desired effect to take place 'lower' down along the ZU-line."

—Crystal Clear (Liber-2B)

Suppressed communication—the inability or unwillingness to extend the reach of communication—tends to result from the assumption of more timid personality characteristics once an individual believes that they will not be understood or that the receipt of their message would be invalidated through laughter, belittling or punishment. Therefore an unwillingness to communicate or extend a creative reach from Self begins to become automatic; and any function of the personal identity system that is running on automatic is running on other-determined control as opposed to Self-determined (assuming of course that the automatic mechanistic relay was not intentionally set up knowingly and intentionally as Self; because then it could be changed, altered or stopped on command).

The reason we introduce the subject of "confront" before "directed application of intention" is because the individual (Pilot or otherwise) must be able to face or direct the intention as a communication *to* some spot in space. True communication is not addressing an empty room or wall— and it is not even addressing an audience. In the case of groups, the directed application of intention is directed between the sender and each individual as a multiplicity.

Often times lack of actualized Self-certainty and fragmentation causes individuals to fail to properly direct their intention; in which case we tend to attack those that speak too softly to hear, address opposite directions from where the receiver is, or are even noticeably hesitant in their delivery of speech to the point where a person must strain to keep their attention. All of these are forms of inadequately directed intention.

Of course, we can just as easily find the other extreme cases where an individual is incessantly loud and unreserved in all manner of channels of speech, even trains of thought that are not relevant to the present situation or a direct response to the communications directed at them. These chaotic flows of energy are not focused and are therefore not under control.

A person who cannot start talking, stop talking or change the flow of direction to be sender or receiver fully at will is not in control of communication or themselves. Much like the operation of a car, ship or other vehicle—the only true applications of Will by the Alpha Spirit as an operator, are to start, stop or alter the direction of motion. These are literally the only fundamental components of control in a system.

Another facet of personal control in both the delivery and receipt of messages involves the added physical expression or efforts attached, which may be distracting or make the flow less clear. These include hand gestures, facial changes, lifting eyebrows, rolling eyes, &tc. An individual in Pilot Training can be observed and reminded that these things are happening, therefore allowing the individual the opportunity to practice specific types of self-control. These automatic mechanisms exist in place of delivering true controlled communication.

A Pilot maintains the integrity of the session using specific methods of controlled communication and specifically designed processing command lines. Failure to maintain control of communication renders the session ineffective for the goals of processing as it degrades into a basic Q-and-A conversation maintained under the control of the Seeker, or at the very least one of their automated mechanistic circuits of communication. Such types of "casual talk" prevent any real processing from occurring.

This type of zigzag shifts the focus of attention on the line among many points or terminals without any direct line back to the actual processing that should be taking place in session. The resulting effect of the communication is always an ongoing feed into the next cycle without actually reaching an understanding or bringing a circuit to a scrutiny.

The following is an example of Q-and-A and poor confronting abilities (the Pilot reacts and changes the session); this is NOT an example of a good communication flow for a systematic session.

PILOT : Imagine the living form of a cat there in front of the body.

SEEKER : I don't like cats.

PILOT : Oh! (*alarm, raised eyebrows, then frown*) What don't you like about cats?

SEEKER : Well, see, they remind me of when I was a child.

PILOT : Did you have a lot of negative experiences as a child?

SEEKER : Its hard to remember my childhood. I don't like to think about it.

PILOT : Would you like to process out some events from childhood?

SEEKER : I was thinking maybe we could just take it easy today.

PILOT : Is there something else you would like to run?

SEEKER : Run? Oh, you know...the last time I was running, you know, jogging down the street, I kept getting this image in my head that I was running a marathon.

PILOT : Have you ever run in a marathon? ...

As you can see, this above conversation is not going anywhere and is far and removed from any kind of effective systematic processing. The Seeker is anxious about something that they are treating as an existing problem—enough to be an interference to the session—than it should be assumed that the problem, at the very least, exists *for* the Seeker. It is a part of their "reality." It is an occurrence or an 'actual thing' taking place in the world.

Whatever the Seeker's present concerns are, and although they may carry some type of fragmentation with them, they are simply treated as a work-a-day issue common to simply being present in society, which may be subject to the considerations of the individual, but are not the actual subject of the session ensuing thereafter. Careers, money, love-life, legal issues... these may all be picking away at the Seeker's attention and bringing their presence away from the session if they are not simply acknowledged at the start. They are simply acknowledged—and that is all. They may not even be tangible problems to be solved; they are whatever the Seeker is carrying with them "off the street." This raises the next subject of discussion for Pilot communication in session, which is the acknowledgment.

Acknowledgment is part of the feedback loop portion of the communication cycle. It is an arc of energy on the comm-line that confirms or validates the very fact that after the original communication point was sent and received, that a response generated has also been received. The Seeker's answer is the validation or acknowledgment of their own receipt of the original communication; otherwise what would they be responding to? However, it is very important that the Seeker receive an acknowledgment of their response in order to close or complete the original circuit. Otherwise the communication cycle is not completed and anything further added to the line will only be adding confusion.

Acknowledgment is a necessary part of true communication if an individual wants to know with certainty that their communication actually arrived at a receipt-point. If you were to throw a ball over a hill in front of you—and therefore to a point out of your actual view—you might hear the ball "hit" something, and lacking a line of sight, that sound would be the acknowledgment that the "point" (ball) traveled a distance and reached its terminal.

Incomplete communication cycles—an answer not given or an acknowledgment not received—are a basis for fragmentation, confusion and an unwillingness thereafter to reach (communicate), at least along certain channels, assuming the individual has not yet generalized all terminals as unworthy of communication. When left to their own devices, this is sometimes the only approach that an individual will take in regards to communication in view of the fact that they have seen poor results of their efforts time and time again. The message that the reactive-response systems send out is "don't bother, nothing's happening."

Systematic Communication Processing assists a Seeker in "tying up" energetic loose ends that have accumulated on various lines. The more incomplete communication cycles extant on a particular line, the more distortion and fragmentation will occur on that line. This "debris" inhibits clear communication between two terminals. One of the techniques employed is to imagine a terminal responding to the Seeker with an acknowledgment, such as "okay." This may even be treated as an additional step toward objective processing.

Acknowledgment is a key component to maintaining control of the communication line; for the Pilot to maintain control of "command lines"; and for a Seeker to stay in session without accumulating more incomplete energetic circuits. Because an acknowledgment is not a prompt to "continue" talking along a circuit, we consider that it is controlling the line by stopping and completing the communication cycle of actions. By acknowledging receipt, we are informing the sender or originator that the intention has been received and they need not keep putting attention on that point. A new cycle may now begin. Even if the utterance is the same, such as in many types of systematic processing, it is still its own cycle of communication and is meant to produce an original response in a separate unit of space-time than the former answer.

The key demonstrated here—and required for the session —is that a person will stop their flow of communication once the acknowledgment has been received. This is important, otherwise the Pilot would lose control of the session and the communication. By letting another person know that their communication has been received you are taking control of the line, because they have completed their action. If no acknowledgment is made, their actions are inclined to go on being applied until an effect has been observed.

Controlled communication is not generally a practiced discipline; seldom even given much significance by the standards of most humans. Most individuals are communicating on automatic circuits that they have set up at one time or another in order to handle inflows from the environment. The Pilot cannot allow automated mechanisms to run rampant throughout the session; and it must be assumed that these are not yet under the Seeker's control or they would be not taking place.

Crudely stated: anything that we may stop or start or even change or alter in some way, we have a certain degree of control over. And this control and the nature of the thing being stopped or started (&tc.) is only a consideration or point-of-view. It is the responsibility of taking control of the lines as a source-point and exercising that Will-Intention on the flow. Now it is true that this is always the case; except however outside of *Self-Honesty*, because if an individual is not in full conscious control of their flows—or the mechanisms they have set up to automate the control— then the *Self* is not in control. So what are we really doing with systematic processing? We are dealing with communication and control of energy and power. No effort has been made to disguise this fact. The Pilot is demonstrating the control and responsibility of the line until the Seeker truly can as *Self*.

One of the first steps is to get a Seeker to realize they are the one *doing* whatever they are doing. This means the Pilot is observant in recognizing the ability level of the individual at the start, and simply selectively directing the

Seeker's attention to that action—whatever it is that they are or can do. If they are simply sitting in the chair, make certain that *they are certain* that *Self* is making that body sit in the chair.

A compulsion is a failure to be responsible for the dynamics of control—starting, stopping or altering—on a particular channel of communication and/or regarding a particular terminal in existence. The flow has an appearance of being stuck however it is already or by the control of some automatic mechanism. As a practice you would start a person intentionally doing what they already do and then show them that the willingness to alter or change directions is their choice by simply demonstrating the opposite dynamic.

For example: an individual who is a compulsive talker may be systematically processed to realize acknowledgments or lack thereof in the physical universe; that would be one technique. Another technique would be a blatant demonstration of control on that channel. So a Pilot says to the Seeker: "When I say the word 'start', you will begin talking and you will continue to talk until I say the word 'stop' and then you will stop speaking, do you understand?"

Of course, we are not suggesting that a few cycles of this will clear a person of all their difficulties, but this is an effective technique that has been found useful. Although the Pilot is appearing to be the director of effect, controlling the line of "start" and "stop," this is not some covert attempt at "making a person do something" or "becoming a robot." A Seeker is awake, they are aware of their presence in the session and they are willingly participating in some demonstration that is found to produce an effective result toward some realization in many instances of its application; if not always, when applied correctly and run completely.

Another aspect that a Pilot will encounter is that most systematic processing involves "duplicating" a command line many times over and over again in succession. This very idea, in traditional society, is the very nature of automation. However, if the Pilot is not able to apply the same actualized intention and Will to the thirtieth time a particular query was used as the first time, then the Pilot too has become nothing more than a machine.

A complete circuit of communication fails blatantly when it is simply not responded to at all. The acknowledgment is part of a receipt of an answer. But if we have not even received an answer to the original question, we do not have a flow of communication. We cannot be certain that the original message was understood or even received. This is very important to know about because it *is* something that will happen in a Piloted session and if it is not handled appropriately, the channels by which the entire session operates on, will begin to become fragmented right there.

When control of communication is not managed in the absence of proper responses and acknowledgments—and yet is still allowed to continue to run noise on the channel—the resulting "conversation" will have no "point" or "direction" and no interested parties will be likely left "interested" in it by then end. No one will have known what anyone else is even talking about. This is what we consider "noise" or interference—or blatantly a "distraction."

A Pilot extends a communication out on the line even when we are using objective processes at the start of a session to orient the Seeker's presence. These are commands or selective directions of attention toward something that the Pilot can actually *observe*. We ask a Seeker to perform a series of basic actions and notice the lag in receiving the command and the ability to transmit the command to a body, and make it do something on command.

An individual following standard-issue human conditioning has become so accustomed to operating on "autopilot" that even these basic steps toward actualization are found to have observable results in increasing an individual's control of their own actions. No matter how basic this all may seem, the full actualized application of Will on the direction of Self worked up on a gradient scale of reach is the only aspect that has ever made other "rituals" and "therapies" even remotely effective.

When a Pilot is operating any of the subjective processes or upper-level techniques, we are dealing with instances when a command line is directed to the Seeker for them to do something within their own personal universe—which is to say imagination and creative imagery using the "Mind's Eye" and eventually total 100% "Spirit Vision" as Alpha/Self. However, it would be impossible to assist a person in performing tasks the Pilot is not able to "see" directly if we cannot even be certain the Seeker can perform the basic tasks that we *can* "see."

Consider the individual that, when asked to perform a task, gives no response, does not perform the task or performs a different task. Consider the confusion that may take place on a line of communication if after asking a question (A), the person is responding to some question (B) from a previous incomplete communication cycle. Even the simple accumulation of unanswered questions and incomplete tasks is enough to cause fragmentation on a line.

Fragmentation is composed of misappropriated *Awareness* (or *Attention*) that is fixed and no longer under the free control of *Self*. This, in a nutshell, is what *all* fragmentation is, whether imprinted as imagery or encoded emotionally or programmed through associative knowledge. It is something left incomplete or misunderstood and so "a part of us" as energy-matter is still left with that anchor point suspended in space-time. You even hear observant people refer to someone like this as being "hung up on something." Whatever it is a person is "hung up" *on*—that individual is "still waiting to receive an answer."

It is extremely important that a Pilot completes every communication cycle before initiating another. As much as this seems evidently practical, it can also be applied to the energetic interactions between ourselves and the entire universe. Repetitive processing methodology is a subject of confusion in Pilot Training because in actuality, we are never repeating or duplicating a previous communication. It does not matter that the same words are used in one command as the former command; the idea that it is actually a "duplicate question" is a false consideration. Communication is only duplicated when a specific point moves across a channel from the source to a receipt point on that channel. A second point with the same characteristics sent along that channel is *not* the "same" point as the first one. That being said, to have the same characteristics it would also have to be carrying the same quality of Will-Intention—without variation—as the first time; which we do observe in proper systematic processing. One consequence of experiencing the standard-issue Human Condition is inability or unwillingness to put any interest into repeated actions... Well, that is one bit of encoding which may be resolved with these skills.

According to the Standard Model, the Physical Universe is commanded and controlled by Will-Intention (5.0) and it is not a point present in *this* physical universe (beta-existence). This means an Alpha Spirit (Self) must direct its intention at a body and then the body will play out the actions attributed to its own physical location. It can be identifiable in space-time as a body and can communicate with other bodies it shares proximity and understanding with in space. If all bodies were potential terminations of a phone line, they would still not be the Self that is holding the receiver at the end and directing the communication.

In modern society, we have put an emphasis on the possession of a body with that of a phone because without these channels we are essentially cut off from the direct experience of communications of reality in the physical universe. But the *Self* is no more a body than it is a phone. It is given value because it is used by *Self* to experience a world of bodies and phones.

When a Pilot is processing a Seeker, they are *not* giving the "same command" over and over again. In fact, each command is its own unit or point of existence carried cross its own arc or curve of space—its own flow on a circuit. It is only when that particular message or command is not received, that an individual will simply begin to put more and more charge on the same flow as the previous time and build up a greater and greater store of personal fragmentation and general confusion.

Most "natural" upper-level successful individuals in society have already gotten a sense of how to manage this. They have learned how to get their questions answered and see their intentions carried out by those they are entrusted to. An individual that is successful in facing terminals in the universe, willing to maintain their own emotional resolve, willing to effectively communicate their intention and acknowledge when attention of others is applied to a flowline to receive it—this is a person that is successful in public life.

:: 8 ::
CONTROL AND RESPONSIBILITY FOR
SELECTIVELY DIRECTED ATTENTION

Ability to command attention is probably one of the more commonly ascribed traits or characteristics to those who are considered successful or charismatic or confident... or dare we say it, "powerful." To what else are we basing our considerations for comparison of such traits if not for the "ability to command attention"? Here then we discover another important key to the success of controlled communication and systematic processing sessions.

It is a lot to ask, given the current state of the human condition, for a Pilot to say, "we will now begin the session" and suddenly everything outside the session goes out of view and the Seeker is "present right there with full attention" (which we call "presence"). Of course, a proper command of the communication line with clear intention would make this possible—and in some respects is a goal—and yet we are not restricting the potential of our methodology to only cases that have already assumed the state of *Homo Novus*. Doing so renders the entire concept of what we are doing for the present state humanity null and void.

An exceptionally low-level of interpersonal communication that may be used by a Pilot—or anyone wishing to establish a communication line with someone at the lower ends of the Beta Awareness Scale—and that is the ability to "Mime" or "Mimic" (and by this, we do not mean mimicry in the antagonistic sense). It may be used as an entry-level step to the selective direction of attention, but only when absolutely necessary.

"Low-Level Systematic Methodology" is more of interest to a Pilot processing a random individual off the street, or even a physician interested in mental science, but not necessarily a Seeker that is actively interested in studying Systemology and carries enough actualized Awareness already to want to "see themselves through" to higher points of beingness. The entire idea of "pushing" the "secret realizations" (intended behind the transmission of these exercises) or even "forcing" processing on someone that does not want to provide their presence to the session is too counter-productive for our intentions. There are plenty of willing Seekers that can benefit from this work.

But to at least provide an example: an individual who cannot at first follow the command to pick up a "bell, book or candle," might be able to mimic an action. You say, "watch what my hand does, okay?" and they should respond in some way—even a facial twinge—to show they got some sense of recognition a message is received. So, you pick up a [bell] and then you ask them, "did you see that?" and if you had their attention before—if you had enough intention on the line for them to look—they will indicate a response.

You can experiment with—and perhaps actualize a few realizations on your own—by trying the most socially recognized example of mimicry out in the world laboratory: "waving your hand" with the intention of "hello." And there you have it. Communication *is* powerful.

Many humans do not maintain control over their attentions; as a result, beta capabilities of the Alpha-Spirit (Will-Intention) get fixed to automatic mechanisms no longer under determination of Self. These functions are resolved as a gradient effort, slowly increasing reach of a Seeker with each new certainty of (or capacity for) ability, hence: "capability." This includes the ability to process "directions."

Keep in mind, we are not asking a Seeker to do anything dangerous; it would seem more dangerous to leave someone in such conditions of fragmentation where they might actually be a danger to self and others by being that "out of touch" with the universe. Unfortunately, this is exactly the state of standard issue human participants. Therefore, control of communication is demonstrated for the Seeker on the body and their attention; then the determination, responsibility and control is gradually returned to the Seeker progressively during the course of processing.

Once a session is begun and a Seeker's presence is established, the two next steps of control involve objective processing and motions/actions of the body. This is as basic as the Pilot directing the attention of the Seeker to "look" at a specific object that is present in space-time. This could graduate into having the Seeker direct themselves to find an object to look at on their own determinism.

Improper management of "control" has led a Seeker to misappropriate responsibility—and therefore control—of the body, the mind, the creative imagery of the mind, and reactivity of the same. Control of these communication lines is passed to some "automated circuit," and this is, at first, willed into action and permanent existence. It remains permanent so long as the responsibility and control of it the mechanism is passed off to some unknown cause or other-determinism.

Greater fragmentation on a line, especially along any specific circuit or toward a specific terminal, is a result of energetic "masses" accumulated rigid imprinting and fixed programming. This will produce greater communication lag from the Seeker while various considerations or barriers are processed through. Often times, the method of using a "repetitive command" is to actually "run out" of all the considerations of a circuit at one level and then have a "breakthrough" in finding a new consideration or definition or perspective on that flow, which then produces a new set of answers.

A Pilot should not rush the Seeker to answer or respond; but the Pilot needs to keep track of the energetic flow and make sure not to add confusion to the line by acting impatient or any other misappropriation of communication. We expect a change in communication lag concerning any particular circuit or terminal as the processing toward defragmentation takes place.

Answers to many questions themselves are not nearly as important as the personal processing used to arrive at them and range of total free consideration available to the Seeker. Answers given may quicken after a lull of reshaping a consideration or altering a definition—but this is left to the Seeker to resolve, because the question or command line proposed is not altered with each cycle in that process. Answers may become scarce if the Seeker is reaching to the "bottom of the bank" concerning something finite.

When a Seeker declares at any time that there are no more answers "coming to Mind" acknowledge ("okay") and continue the session. If the channel still requires defragmentation (but nothing else may be "recalled"), a Pilot's additional route available is having the Seeker "imagine" various scenarios and the practice of **"thought experiments"** on a channel, which may also lead to the optimum actualized realization.

It is every human's responsibility to learn to handle communication, control and commands because of how much they have a tendency to fragment daily life with their common use. It is in our benefit that we may systematically use these same channels to "undo" the fragmentation that exists on the lines. Our proper handling of communication during sessions and in everyday life is the key to resolving the problems of the human condition. Here we point out that "commands" are impressed onto the systems of the personal identity continuum at a relay point—which are indicated specifically on the Standard Model as the:

"ACC" – Alpha Control Center; (7.0) on the Standard Model

"MCC" – Master Control Center; (4.0) on the Standard Model

"RCC" – Reactive Control Center; (2.0) on the Standard Model

These are abstract in relation to our experience of solids in the physical universe when compared to (1.0) at the bio-chemical level and (0.0) as the inert material continuity of condensed energies in the physical universe. However, these are not any less "real." The RCC has, in the original presentations of systemology a decade ago, been equated to a Mind-of-the-Body, running on reactive-response mechanisms that control automated functions of the body. This semantic is simply in contrast to the MCC, which was formerly considered as the Mind-of-the-Spirit.

The MCC *is actually not* the Mind-of-the-Alpha-Spirit, but it is the uppermost level of "Mind" that is still connected to the human condition. The Mind is actually a bridge between the influence of the Will (from a higher order of Alpha existence) and what is treated as the control centers and functions of the physical body, which are governed by the RCC. It is the interaction of the Alpha Spirit with the systems of the genetic vehicle or organic entity that creates a field of relay between them, that we consider the Mind.

For example, we may demonstrate the entire design and makeup of a genetic entity as controlled by reactive-response mechanism at (2.0). In theory, this means that independent of the Will from an Alpha-Spirit, a living organism would function at its most basic level of survival needs solely by the RCC.[*]

There are some systemologists that have often referred to this reactive control center as the "animal mind" or "primitive mind" because some presumed it to be the limit of intelligence of "conscious life" short of being imbued by some additional element of "divine consciousness." This is not entirely the case; it is simply the way in which the relay control centers seem to be wired in appearance when compared to standard-issue knowledge about "life." Animals demonstrate a greater capacity than the RCC alone—and so, the RCC is simply the extent of the genetic cellular

---

[*] Refer to *"The Tablets of Destiny"* and *"Crystal Clear"*—also contained in the Grade-III *"Systemology Handbook."*

stimulus-response inherited in a physical form. It is also established that a spiritual entity controlling a body can "step out of that POV" and still leave the body as a living and breathing organism running on its own most basic functions. Some believe this is what happens when we sleep.

Causally, communication is always a means of producing effect—but the fact that it may be "wired" directly to points of fragmentation is a concern. Because then, all someone would need to do is know our "**hot buttons**" to be able to control us; thereby usurping the Will of the Alpha-Spirit by engaging a direct line on the RCC. The Alpha-Spirit would be helpless but to watch the games of the body play out without their control. This is actually what happens for the human condition when the Self no longer maintains responsibility and control of communication lines with the physical universe. If not *you*, then *who?*

Many individuals that are fragmented by improper handling of control have a difficult time demonstrating "self-control"—failing even this, they go on to find ways to enforce control on others. Keep in mind, this is the same individual that is not demonstrating the ability to have their own best spiritual, mental and physical interests in line. This all provides a finite number of conditions of control an individual could be in:

a) maintaining actualized control as Self on the personal identity continuum and knowing it;

b) maintaining no actualized control as Self and having functions of the RCC or Mind-Systems operated by some other-determined cause; and

c) maintaining an actualized conscious agreement for the function of the RCC or Mind-Systems to be operated by a Pilot for purposes of systematic processing.

This breaks down roughly to: being aware one is in control; not being aware one is not in control; and being aware that one is not in control. In *Grade-III*, we stated similar conditions about *Awareness*: being aware that one is aware, not being aware... and so on. On a systematic level, we find just a few of these basic states of control and system dynamics at work. It is the combination of just a few dynamics at work that creates a functioning system.

There are several conditions that may be fragmented in an individual, which when brought to light in this education, will be found to strongly affect the Pilot-in-Training, and also the quality of processing an individual would bring to a session. These matters are all part of an Alpha-Spirit's considerations; they have no other true moral implication other than what is associated to them as an imprint and then as erroneous programming. Consider then:

> the willingness to control others;
> an inability to control others; and
> the compulsion to control others.

An individual agreeing to processing in session is therefore providing a presence of willingness to "play the game" of "systematic processing."

Of course, Willingness is a quality of the intention supplied into the physical control centers of the Mind-Systems. These share a systematic and dynamic relationship with the RCC and reactive-response mechanisms of the body. This is important to understand because of phenomenon that may take place during processing, when a Seeker is suddenly "unwilling" or has hit a "blockage."

Let us assume for a moment that when uninhibited, not in a state of fragmented stimulation, and free to decide on the course of actions, has decided to pursue a study of Systemology, proceeds to read through the *Systemology Handbook* and various course manuals and decides that this is actually something they are interested in doing. Where then should we place cause when the same Seeker is suddenly resisting and opposing their progress in a session?

We might be left to wonder very quickly if we have made an error as Pilots. This is assuming we have not considered that the difficulties a Seeker is having in controlling the body is not restricted to a few isolated incidences, but is actually deeply ingrained in their fragmentation, imprints, programming and self-created mechanisms (automated machinery).

Past imprinting concerning control, communication and responsibility are just as likely to hangup a Pilot that has not achieved an actualized beta state of Self-Honesty and is not in a position of Self-control themselves. Quite frankly: ministers, instructors and Pilots are "drilled" on skills much harder and more rigorously than the average Seeker or student experiences, approaching this field of study, philosophy and spirituality from the other side. One of the reasons is because the Pilot is also a Seeker, or starts off as a Seeker, and here we are delivering manuals that essentially have answer keys within them that bring to light some of the most coveted esoteric realizations from over 6,000 years of recorded history...but they are still being *read*, not *realized*.

A Pilot that has not started their own journey as a Seeker being processed from a point of naivete, has not had the opportunity to reach these same realizations on their own through processing. This means that we have to substitute the attainment of realizations from the systematic processes themselves as a form of demonstration. The Pilot is given the unique opportunity to see the fundamental systemology of all *Life, the Universe and Everything* play out right before themselves in every application of processing —and even during training, with the intellectual consideration and "thought-experiments" possible, simply by working through the manuals—and previous *Grade-III* materials. A certainty of things *will* develop.

Education and training in Mardukite Zuism and Systemology Technology is an application of a precision spiritual philosophy to all *Life, the Universe and Everything*. It is not exclusively a field of training for "Pilots" conducting *Professional Piloting Procedure*; such is only one avenue of direct application, and yes, an official one within the capacity of our work as a "group organization" that delivers materials, educational training and spiritual services.

The individual that has achieved a beta state of Self-Honesty is an individual with the ability to confront—face up to—and thus communicate on all channels of *Life, the Universe and Everything*. Whether trained with recognition and a fancy-lettered certificate or trained within the confines of one's own residence, the principle tools and skills administered under the banner of Mardukite Zuism and NexGen Systemology may be applied "out of session" in the world-at-large with considerable benefit. To restrict an application of this knowledge in any other way is to limit it to the very boundaries that it has proposed to resolve.

:: 9 ::
RESPONSIBILITY FOR CONTROL AND
COMMAND OF MIND-BODY COMMUNICATIONS

Fragmentation is reinforced by validation of the RCC (reactive control center) as the command center of the body. Unfortunately, this is one issue with overuse of *cathartic processing* (Route-1 methods) as the sole means of resolving personal turbulence: it repeatedly validates the mechanistic functions of the RCC. Yet, all upper-level knowledge is still true at a *Grade-IV* level of understanding: the Alpha-Spirit, having become more and more engrossed by the data and masses identifying Self with beta-existence then discovers itself (or never discovers this point) that they have become entrapped within—or are suddenly barred by—only the mechanistic considerations of *Life, the Universe and Everything*, following only a nature of the "machines" it has witnessed as "reality" at this lower-level of fragmentary and condensed physical existence.

The truer nature of reality and existence is far more fluid. The ability to change and alter flows of energy; to start and stop the motion of any system; to create and dissolve universes; all of this lies at the upper reaches of spiritual existence that lies outside the domain or realm of this physical existence. According to the Arcane Tablets, these two basic distinctions of existence are separated and defined by the LAW, which sealed physical existence away from spiritual existence.

To the extent to which we may determine anything with certainty, we can be sure that an Alpha Spirit begins to associate the identity (and nature) of Self with a physical body and the senses of the physical body. In this instance it is not treated as a "genetic vehicle" but as a consideration of the totality of Self, right there in-and-as the body. This is the only consideration that can even logically promote the existence of a "finite afterlife" which is contrary knowledge to what we know to be true. If you are to go to a "heaven" for all eternity after a lifetime, how would you live again? And how did you live before? These are contradictory considerations and are a perfect example of the cognitive dissonance that emerges from fragmentation. Only by the Alpha-Spirit considering that they are the body can they be affected by the body. Otherwise there is no other real access point for fragmentation to the "true" Self.

Until the Alpha-Spirit makes the consideration (and reality-agreement) that what happens to the body will in some way affect the I-AM, there is no real concern about the events that one is experiencing. The ability to confront and face-up to all terminals in the universe is simply an ability to share communication and let everything pass through as a wave without putting up blocks and other points of strain on the line.

We are very active creative beings, but until we can handle and manage the reactivity of the experience of our creations, we are not in a command position of control and responsibility. This is what defines the states of actualization—and to the extent by which a spirit is both willing and able to reach. If we can consider the ALL without the limits of the mechanistic LAW, then we have *really* stepped outside the box into Alpha Thought. Even a fragmented individual not yet beta-actualized can be brought to a realization that these points of fragmentation—when examined on the Standard Model—do not actually affect the nature of Self at (7.0); they impinge upon the personal identity continuum that one is attending to (has attention on).

It may be assumed (though not treated at these beta levels of knowing) that since the Infinity of Nothingness (8.0) is likely to produce an equal infinity of all wave crests of I-AM peaks—at (7.0)—that the Alpha-Spirit at this state may very well be connected on a line to more than one personal identity continuum operating in beta-existence; and this may very well account for multiple lives, or perhaps even all possible lifetimes, each still operating independently on their own existential timeline. We are, of course, most concerned with the one presently knowingly using sensory faculties of a body to read this book, or the one sitting in front of us as a Seeker. We are here now because apparently this is what has significance; this is where it *is* at.

We have been led to believe that the human condition is very "mysterious" and that there is nothing that we can truly know about it; because of course, it's all theory, and mostly all self-serving information anyways—used by one authority to prove a point, then changed and altered to prove a completely different point. This is what we have discovered as "progress" among the conventional scientific community ever since it was able to resume its work after the Dark Ages of Roman Christianity. It has never returned to an apex of its former Golden Age of intellectual and spiritual balance.

The challenge in applying *Professional Piloting Procedure* to a session—or even the manner of handling communications in the everyday world—concerns selecting the appropriate channel and applying the right intensity. A Pilot should master a full understanding of the *Beta Awareness Scale* and corresponding *Emotimeter* of the human condition in order to assess the status of a Seeker during processing, or anyone that you in tend to communicate with.[*]

Keep in mind that an individual is meant to run through an entire course of reactivity in a circuit with a terminal, and the intensity will be felt to the degree that a circuit is fragmented. Once the line is defragmented, a Seeker has no difficulty maintaining responsibility and control of the communication of energy on that line—and that is what we call "true power." A reader that is not yet as familiar with the Standard Model, the *Zu-line*, *Beta-Awareness Scale* or *Emotimeter* can simply treat the material of this book on

---

[*]   The *Beta-Awareness Scale* and *Emotimeter* are fully described in *Crystal Clear*, and in the Grade-III *"Systemology Handbook."*

a gradient of fragmentation. Energy comes into the system at (4.0) and this is considered full *beta-Awareness*. To the extent that the energy is allowed to have a clear pathway to travel toward the continuity of the physical universe (0.0), there is no fragmentation on the line and there is an "honest" POV (point-of-view or viewpoint) accessible from Self.

Between (4.0) and (0.0) we find the entire system of the human condition. An ideal state is to operate this human condition from a point of actualized *Awareness* that is "exterior" to the system, where the Self actually relies in its Alpha condition; however, the more an individual has decided to operate from lower POVs on the line, the more fixed and rigid those points become and there is no room for higher considerations. Reality has been fixed to the experiences on the line from a certain point down to (0.0) and it is within this new range or band of considerations that we would say a Seeker is stuck.

If a Pilot were able to determine the point at which an individual has fixed or stuck their beliefs along a certain channel, this would be of benefit. Well, this is actually the entire purpose behind the *Beta-Awareness Scale* (and even the administration of the *Beta-Awareness Test*)*—to determine a chronic state. A Pilot should be familiar with the *Grade-III* materials concerning *Awareness* because they are likely to encounter an entire array of expression from a Seeker during a process that has a lot of imprinted energy-stores on it—of which we would say that the line is heavily "charged"—or it is a "hot button" as some of the younger systemologists assisting research at the offices often refer to it as.

(4.0) "Vibrancy" – feelings of accomplishment and great success of triumph over life's challenges; a new realization or achievement of knowing and beingness; full operation of Mind-Systems; local presence and control of the physical body.

---

* The *"Beta-Awareness Test"* (*BAT*) is described in *Crystal Clear*.

(3.5) "Outgoing" – pointed speech and focused attention; very directed with intention; confident and positive in outlook of future application of ability; the minimum expectation (condition) for defragmentation of an energy current, session, &tc.

(3.0) "Content" – friendly disposition and engages in casual conversation with attention and interest on the comm line, session or processing; best results for progressive or effective communication, especially in processing, are conducted at least at this level of interest and control, even if not their chronic state (or BAT score); at (3.0) a Seeker has reached a point of only 50% present-time beta-Awareness.

Lower levels of actualized session presence (*Awareness*) below 3.0 actually require a greater emphasis on "control processing" to elevate a Seeker to higher "Session Awareness" (SA). Session Awareness is treated separately from a BAT score or an interpretation of an individual's chronic state. Personal actualized *Awareness*—and control over the Mind–Body system—drops to lower points on our abstract scales and models as more barriers and solids are imposed on an individual during their lifetime, and particularly as they are imposed or added onto the channel or circuit to any terminal as fragmentation.

Desire to improve ability is present at lower-levels of beta-thought but too often overshadowed by indoctrination, encoding and repeated enforcement along some channel. So much invalidating communication has been received from others in these circuits that it becomes too difficult—or out of the willingness to reach—to maintain high levels of personal determinism.

(2.5) "Tolerant of Existence" – ranging from such states as dismissive of a subject to being completely bored; present in body, but otherwise marginally occupied with an interest in exercising personal Will-Intention on the environment.

If a Pilot is successful in delivering such an individual to higher levels of communication and actual get their attention focused in the session as a presence, then the individual is increasing the handling of *Awareness* and more "content" with their environment (3.0). However, if the Seeker has a significant amount of distortion on a line and it begins to trigger "sensations" or "somatic discomfort" then less *Awareness* is being applied to the management of personal reality and the they will go into a point of "invalidation"—which we register as (2.0) on the scale simultaneous with the RCC.

(2.0) "Invalidating" – uncomfortable with the environment, mental images and facets incited by the environment; an individual that is experiencing turbulence along one of their lines/channels of communicative energy and exhibiting suspicion of the session, the intentions of the Pilot and a general pessimism about the processing.

"Session Awareness" (SA) begins with a Pilot's encounter with the Seeker "at the door" and not necessarily the "start" of session. We are, of course, gauging the communication level and presence of the Seeker in session; after this, SA fluctuates during the session based on whatever fragmentation is being processed (imprints, programming, &tc) or whatever RCC line, channel or circuit is being run.

If we consider "boredom" on the spectrum of potential reactivity to a terminal circuit, it is actually up in the range of mental beta-thought, albeit low-energy levels of thought. Yet, when we compare even this to the alternatives engaged by the RCC, the state of boredom would be an amazing achievement *forward* in responding to a terminal than any of the lower emotional states of pain, anger, sadness and apathy. In this instance, processing a line of experience that formerly incited personal feelings of rage and sadness to a point of "boredom" would be, in itself, the most therapeutic phenomenon some people might ever have the opportunity to experience in their lifetime—

and we are certainly not limiting the potential effects of systematic processing to be a state of "boredom."

When presence drops below a state of boredom, the direct line of *Awareness* to Self is withdrawing its actualized Will and as a result we see a general increasing "withdrawal" of the "spirit" from the "body," as it descends into lower and lower levels of emotional solidity.*

Once a Seeker is accustomed to systematic processing procedures and is readily able to "be" in session with their presence, then it becomes easier to start working directly with terminals that are likely to be in stimulation immediately after the session has ended. That being the case, it is better to improve a Seeker's own basic state of certainty concerning Self-determinism before having hours of processing effort immediately nullified by subjecting them to the same circumstances that they are still developing the willingness and reach to manage. For this reason, in special instances, a Seeker may wish to at least temporarily relocate away from certain terminals in life while developing the certainty to face them. It does not work out well for a Seeker that is receiving a daily dose of invalidation while working toward a greater state of knowing and beingness.

All control of the Mind-Systems (MCC) and genetic vehicle/entity (RCC) are a matter of Alpha Thought (6.0)— pure consideration that is directed into *beta-experience* of the human condition (via Will). Relay across the other control systems follows but it is now beyond the proximity of Will-Intention (5.0). It is important then to return control of the automated machinery and the reactive-response mechanisms to the Seeker. For some who are not very actualized, the very idea of the ability to "change your mind" seems too superficial to be important. Those with a lot of "gum in the works" are not experiencing clear communication as the Alpha-Spirit with its own

---

* Refer to *"The Tablets of Destiny Revelation"* (*Liber-One*); also contained in the complete Grade-III *"Systemology Handbook."*

spectrum/continuum as an identity.

One important necessary part of "two-way communication" is quite simply: getting your question answered. As such, we are using systematic processing methods that use repetitive questions, though each is issued in its own cycle as its own unit or point or bit of data being transmitted independently of any other. It is not a "repeat" of a command formerly just given or a build upon a previous answer. It is the same words used to issue a new processing command line, which is brought to a finality. The communication lag is not simply an interval of time in getting any response, but literally the period of time that passes before the actual answer to the original question manifests.

PILOT : (*Original Question*) What's your name?

SEEKER : (*lag*) I can't believe the traffic today and how long it took to get here.

PILOT : I understand. Now, what is your name?

SEEKER : (*lag*) That's a funny word—"name."

PILOT : Okay. (*Thank You*) Now, what is your name?

SEEKER : (*Answers*) Oh— ...it's John.

PILOT : Thank you. (*Question 2*) What's your name?

SEEKER : (*lag. pause, data blockage, fragmented processing*)

PILOT : Okay. I will repeat the command line. (*Repeat Q2*) What's your name?

SEEKER : (*Answers*) It's John.

PILOT : Thank you. Now, just to be sure—What's your name? (*Q3*)

SEEKER : (*Answers*) John.

PILOT : (*Acknowledgment*) Thank you.

Whether piloting an airplane, a spaceship, Self or a Seeker, all of the control and communication requires the certainty and determination to manage space and time—and for purposes of specifically piloting: the environment of the session, the status/location of Pilot and the status/location of the Seeker.

Actualized control via Self-honest management with certainty means the ability to accelerate, decelerate or change direction—all of which are descriptions of the actions, motions and flows of any system. It does however apply very well to the analogy of piloting a ship or the control of a vehicle or the handling of processing or handling of energetic flows—the beauty of working from the systemological paradigm is that the same principles apply across the boards of all systems.

In applied systemology where "Piloted processing" is extant, the focus on control pertains to the direction of attention. Ability to determine control of a "body"/"ship" toward a destination where a Seeker finds themselves rehabilitated in their control of self-determinism, is a matter of controlling attentions. The control of personal attention is the key to applying the power of personal Awareness and the Observer-Effect onto existence in the universe. This is how an individual is made to "agree" to something or is imprinted about the meaning of what things are. There is always someone along to come tell us what and how things *are*.

As communication lags get shorter and control over the body and the responses become more direct, the entry-level processes do not have to be run on an individual as long. This means that while some basic Mind-Body control processing might be introduced at the beginning of every session, these techniques would not necessarily need to be run very long before the Seeker would achieve the same result that a previous session may have spent a greater amount of time on.

For example, if the first few sessions of a Seeker's official piloted journey on the Pathway to Self-Honesty each involve 30-60 minutes of basic objective processing and Mind–Body circuit control, it is very possible that after clearing these circuits, such an exercise would require less and less time at the beginning of later sessions to produce the same results, which then puts the Seeker in a better position to spend session time on successively higher levels of processing. All of which is conducted on a gradual scale of operation.

In other mystical and esoteric applications of personal development, the same type of cumulative gains might be equated to the ability to work on some type of preliminary ritual or meditation prerequisite whereby the first time an hour is spent properly visualizing some symbol as solid in the air; the next time the symbol and a circle around the area where one is sitting; then the next time the individual would be able to add more steps to the same period of time because the ability to conjure a symbol and a circle would only require a smaller portion of the time to concentrate attentions on and make real in the Mind's Eye with a consideration.

This is the type of gradient you would find in some "magical" development program whereby an initiate must be able to visualize more and more solid symbols in a shorter period of time while also conducting various actions and gestures. The effectiveness of any of this is the initiate having spent time mastering the ability to consider and create the parts—each individually—and then be able to summon a reality on them collectively much quicker and stronger than before.

Attention is a powerful tool for Self—and others seem to instinctively know this. It is the direct conduit to our flow of energy, which follows our attention. When an individual applies attention and interest along any line, channel or circuit, they are validating both the nature of the circuit and the terminal it is connected to. This is how things are given their reality.

Simply by directing attention to what others present as something as an *is*, we are offering our own agreements to that "thing" as an *is*. Whatever it *is*, whatever it is determined to be, the energetic line simply follows. Experience of the *is* will always be validated by personal data in combination with the personal interest and attention levels.

As we analyze and consider what something *is*, it becomes more and more our own. In fact, this is what many people refer to as an "idea." If an individual loses the ability to direct their own attention and the ability to control emotional reactions connected to the circuit on that line of attention, then it will be found that the line itself—or whoever is managing the other end of the line or access to the "button"—is given all the causal control and responsibility and the individual will consistently assume a victim-phase when encountering it.

The dialogue given previously is illustrative only. There are many points of it that are bad practice. The main fault with actual application of the script in real life is that the Pilot did not handle the present concerns of the Seeker before putting them into a directed line of communication. The Seeker is still brushing off the emotional residue of navigating through traffic to get there on time and the Pilot is only partially acknowledging this fact.

Another major concern is that a Pilot must be certain if what a Seeker says is actually the Seeker saying it or if there is a "language imprint" somewhere on the line that is in stimulation. When individuals reach certain emotional levels and/or they reach out and touch the wires on a certain circuit to a terminal, they may go into a reactive-response manifestation on language channels. They simply start an encoded "recording" of pre-programmed thoughts and various self-talk "commands" on a circuit.

One goal of systematic processing is for the Seeker to be able to differentiate their knowing and assignment of significance. There is a wide sweeping difference between Self-determination and the "buttons" linking automated response mechanisms to erroneous programming and a fixation on what is no longer in control or held with responsibility. Increasing the Seekers ability and certainty to be Self-determined resolves many of the automatic functions that inhibit actualized *Awareness* as an Alpha (spiritual) being.

The standard-issue human condition is fragmented. The ability to *be* and direct personal experience is too often controlled and dictated by another authority—until an individual's agreements finally resolve in setting up automated machinery, because systematically it is the most effective way to resolve delivering the same conditioned responses without having to place any higher-level personal intention into it. Even the genetic vehicle is wired this way at a cellular level.

The ability to *know* or *think* is also subject to considerable authoritarian control for the average Human. The irony is that whatever is considered or postulated as fact from within the standard-issue condition of humanity is likely not to be an individual *thinking* for themselves any time that one of their "buttons" is activated. As a result we cannot say that the *actions* exhibited in the Physical Universe are solely efforts triggered by Alpha Will-Intention if the individual is heavily fragmented. Energetic blockages on the line literally inhibit the transmission of clear communication between Self and the control of the body.

In *NexGen Systemology*, "mental blockages" are treated as communication lines that have been imprinted or encoded or heavily charged with emotion and condensed as a kind of mass. In earlier *Grade-III* materials, we refer to this as "belief," and it has been written by modern philosophers that "Belief Imparts Reality"—which means it is up to an individual to decide what something *is* and what meaning and significance it should have. Even in mythologies, an ability to "name" physical existence and "classify" experience was the first "sentient" quality that allowed humanity to commandeer Spaceship Earth.

:: 10 ::
THE ENERGY AND TRUE POWER OF SELECTIVELY DIRECTED ATTENTION

There is little reason in putting a lot of intellectual emphasis on fancy words and definitions to describe *attention*. As far as we can tell, it is an inherent knowingness that we are aware of as *consciousness*. This is one aspect that does not require being taught about (although we seem to benefit from a reminder as we go further on in our 'years') since it is the very thing that all living beings have an innate sense of. They have an attention they are directing as a focus, or which is being demanded by some authority or distraction, and there is an inherent *knowing* attached to the experience that we are directing our personal energy wherever our attention lands.

As a child discovers this, they also realize there is a benefit to having those attentions; they can inherently feel the energy that accompanies it because they are still that sensitive—have not projected a bunch of screens and filters through which to view life yet—and they learn ways of managing it. When it is not received through one or more productive efforts than an effect will be earned some other way, and the naïve child begins to "act out" because they want their beingness as an identity validated with "attentions."

If we examine all *Life, the Universe and Everything*—we discover our "attention" *is* valuable. In fact, it is so valuable that it has been likened to our very spiritual life-force energies by many mystics and sages of the past. And as soon as we find ourselves locked into a world of sensory fragmentation, the demands on attention become great—more and more of the system seeks validation; everyone wants the certainty to know that they exist.

There is certainly no shortage of energies running rampant, flowing all throughout the world in every which direction. Those who constantly speak in references of being "depleted in energy" or "cannot focus" or "always tired" or "can't seem to get things done"—all of this stems from the inability to properly recognize and manage the energetic continuity that is taking place all around us at all times.

Some time spent directing personal attention around a room or at various objects at Will is not simply an exercise used by a Pilot to manage controlled communication— there is actual energetic value in many types of objective processing that increases the flow (and personal certainty of managing the flow at will) of clear communications between Self and any and all terminal-circuits of attention maintained with the physical universe or another living being.

All focused selectively directed attention—whether Self-determined, demanded/enforced, distracted by a "button" &tc.—carries personal ZU-energy—or Actualized Aware-ness—into the cycles and systems of manifestation de-scribed throughout "NexGen Systemology." These systems —as demonstrated on our Standard Models and Charts—

carry "Alpha Thoughts" (6.0) as "Will-Intention" (5.0)

from "Spiritual Beingness" (*spiritual consciousness*)

into "Mental Knowingness" (*mental consciousness*)

where it is carried into—and realized for—

the Physical Universe by the "beta-Thought" (4.0) of a

"beta-Lifeform" connected on the ZU-line ("*Identity*").*

From this degree of Self-direction on downward, it is the MCC (Mind-System) that is responsible for gauging "Ef-fort" necessary to enact the desired change/manifestation in the Physical Universe—and it is generally "correct" to the degree that it is defragmented and actualized.

It is not difficult to understand at this juncture, perhaps, the meaning behind the statement that: "best intentions

---

* Excerpting "*Crystal Clear*"; also in the *Systemology Handbook*.

are not enough to gain desired results." Validation of "Alpha Thought" (6.0) and Self-direction of "Will-Intention" (5.0) are very significant demonstrations of our higher levels of beingness and knowingness. Yet, at the same time, we can easily see how, as this communication signal travels "down" the conduit of the personal identity continuum and solidifies (lowers) its frequency, other relay centers are required to properly cycle and "channel" energies to the extent that these "channels" are free and clear of fragmentation.

The mystery of life is therefore maintained by not being able to apply our attentions appropriately at Will. Other erroneously associated data and programming can also encode a fixed imprint on the line of a specific channel. We can, in essence, allow ourselves to see no further past the point we don't understand—and those facets and terminals with significances we don't understand are simply those which we do not have a controlled communication with or the ability to fix and unfix our attention upon by Will. What else is the Alpha-Spirit even "directing" in *beta-existence* when acting "Self-directed"?—if not the application of their own energies by controlling the flow via selective attention.

The cliché statements about being "afraid of what we don't understand" and "only fearing fear itself" have not brought humanity to any higher realization on the handling of personal attention and the right communication necessary to "understand" anything. In many cases an individual is energetically treating any aspect that they are not willing to face or handle as the "darkness," the "distortion," the "distraction" and the "unknown" simply by a basic unwillingness to confront, communicate and understand. Once these images and their facets are turned into unknowns, they are attended to with fear and dislike mechanisms.

That the original channel and true data remains extant underneath the nature of all "personal mystery" is a strange phenomenon. Just because a person has thrown up a filter on a channel, or attended the dark screens and mysterious "blacknesses" with fear, does not mean that there is not actual information still in play for this game of which we are simply not seeing.

Mishandling of energy and communication; the formation of blockages, barriers, filters and mechanisms; attending things we don't understand with our energy and *Awareness*; all of these actions actually contribute to making what is already misaligned even more solid and rigidly fixed in place as a consideration—even when the moment when that consideration was agreed to and fixed in place is forgotten.

When we consider the "magician" conducting a ritual, every single aspect of the ceremonial demonstration is meant simply to selectively direct attention. The illusion and trapping of the lower Grades of "magic" lies in the consideration that some otherwise inaccessible power is concealed through the utterance of a secret word at the appropriate time when such and such planet is visible in the sky and the initiate is standing on one foot hopping about the circle nine times backwards trying not to trip on a series of magical tools laid out in the four directions as they swing a wand in their right hand and making certain to keep the incense censor fed with the left hand, lest they be able to catch a breath of real fresh oxygen and begin to wonder what they are doing this whole time.

This is not meant to invalidate personal realizations and gains of self-determined certainty that are equally possible at the *Grade-I* and *Grade-II* designations of magic instruction, mysticism, religion and hermetic philosophies.[*] However, when the magician displaces the "source and cause" of Will to other-determined responsibilities, an "out of the box" paradigm serves only to entrap an initiate

---

[*]   Refer to Grade-I and Grade-II Master Editions—"*The Great Magickal Arcanum*," "*Merlyn's Complete Book of Druidism*," and "*Necronomicon: The Complete Anunnaki Legacy.*"

in another, different or larger "box."

Fixing a line of attention is very similar to fixing attention on a line of communication, and when this is controlled properly, amazing things can happen. Ability to selectively direct and fix attention (and really really fix it well) is what we attribute to the "power to create." And there is no higher faculty that we have discovered for Self other than the ability to freely consider and be willing to create —which is only actualized to the degree that one is willing to take responsibility for creations as cause. When they are attributed to some other-determined cause, the power and energy attached to the creation is surrendered—and yet the individual still remains very much connected to the solidity of the creation.

Fixation on an issue or problem limits the scope of Attention that an individual is willing to apply—and thus limits the amount of actualized *Awareness* that is given to control of the personal identity continuum and functions of the Mind-System: to be able to change, at Will, the ideas, thoughts, considerations, postulates and mental image creations.

As a Seeker works through *Grade-III* and *Grade-IV* type systematic processing and systemological education, the realizations demonstrate that we are increasing the "apparent ability" of the individual by increasing the span of potential uninhibited thought activity—thereby freeing it from its erroneous associations and reactive-response mechanisms. Much of this is handled directly with "systematic subjective processing," which is then alternated with the more "objective processes" that allow an individual to reclaim and recycle the stores of mental energy that have been managed during a "subjective" exercise.

It may be stated that the focus of subjective processing is aimed specifically at a Seeker's thought activity, conceptions, considerations and significances attached thereto. They are exercises, usually elevated to an analytical level, that address the *knowingness* maintained by the Self, or at least the present awareness as Self. This is also comparable to where attention is fixed. In contrast, objective processing focuses on an increased awareness toward control of what the Self is *doing*, which is also to say: energy that is directed onto the attention line. This basic systemology of function is where we discover the compartments of Self-identity; a spirit that is *being*; a mind that is *knowing* and a body that is *doing*; however these are relayed.

An individual may very well have been strongly conditioned, deeply emotionally encoded along some channel to simply no longer want to recognize it or look at it—its power and energy has become so fixedly designated as inhibiting and destructive and the individual no longer wants anything to do with it. This leads to later considerations that "this is bad" and "that is pain" and "I don't want to know" and of course ultimately, "I don't want to be responsible for control and energy and power because it is bad and painful and I want nothing to do with it as cause so I will be the effect because I cannot change it then and I don't have to be responsible for damage and pain which now someone else has caused to me..." This is not an Alpha-Spirit talking, thinking, or acting in a Self-determined fashion at all.

One technique—that many spiritual philosophies have each developed their own versions of—concerns the ability to "imagine problems" or literally "create problem scenarios" in the mind that Self knows that they are creating and of which they can apply some attention to. If it is closely similar to the original channel or terminal-circuit, then all the better. If a Pilot can get the Seeker to consider similar problems to the one that they are overwhelmed with, new realizations can result and a greater certainty for solving problems in general.

Problems are not inherently bad—much like everything else—and an individual is likely to respond or handle them as they would any terminal-circuit to the extent that such channel is clear of fragmentation. Even delivery of a communication requires solving problems; and an individual will always be found solving a problem about something—whether or not they are fixed, obsessed and operating on automation is the other matter altogether.

Presence is "personal orientation of Self or POV located in space-time and handling the energy-matter present in the environment"—so that is a condition we want to make sure is present before the actual start of a session. Keep in mind that the preliminary steps of Piloting are drawn from the same methodology that others use improperly to cause fragmentation; for example, as "social programming" and what some refer to as conditioning—this is accomplished with four basic steps (which we then actually handle more responsibly in *Professional Piloted Procedure* than we are to expect that a Seeker has had the opportunity to experience in the normative standard-issue world-at-large).

1. get into communication on a channel
2. maintain control of the communication line
3. demonstration (of communication and control)
4. widening (or fixing) of considerations (beliefs)

Information within Systemology—materials contained within esoteric Grades and the applied practical philosophies of *Grade-III* and *Grade-IV*—is only "dangerous" if it remains suppressed below common knowledge. It is only "dangerous" when it remains exclusively in the hands of upper-level echelons of society—and too often such individuals use the knowledge only to impose more barriers on the public, producing more and more personal fragmentation by way of erroneous enforcement.

Knowledge that is researched, discovered, experimented with and demonstrated throughout *NexGen Systemology* is only "new" to those individuals being permitted access to the secret wisdom for the first time. The truth is that Systemology and systematic processing is not based on "new" information that suddenly developed out of nowhere, but it does take a more practical approach to esoteric knowledge contained on the Arcane Tablets—even more practical and direct than many of the quasi-mystical magical orders and "secret societies." Such organizations have already been in possession of some reflection of this knowledge for thousands and thousands of years since the **Ancient Mystery School**.

An individual applies their "attention" to such subjects, objects and environments that are equivalent to their level of interest. Obviously a person will give more attention to the things they are interested in—including the terminals of "magic" or "religion" or "spirituality." A person is likely only to give such things attention if they are demonstrated to have some level of relevancy for daily life. Other individuals may not even be aware that their interests in such things as "wizard-dragon fantasy" and "science-fiction space-opera" are most likely resonant energies connected to flows on channels to "past lives" and "past life memory."[*]

The power of attention may be summed up to be: "the consideration of Self to selectively direct its own *Awareness* as a focal point on any line, which is to say a point in space." The actual consciousness of an individual that is so often fixed and tied only to the considerations and *Awareness* as a physical body, is able to be transferred at Will by Self to any other point that it can consider in space—and if there isn't a point in space, the Alpha-Spirit creates it simply by the consideration that it is there, and fixes attention on it.

Understanding the physical universe has been a great strain on the standard-issue human condition, because as a form wired solely to sensory information about the tangibles and solids of existence, the entire background reality to *Life, the Universe and Everything* has completely eluded the semantic-set and vocabulary of most convent-

---

[*] Such subjects are treated at higher *Grades* of Systemology and upper-levels of systematic processing. In the meantime, a Pilot emphasizes Awareness and responsibility in *this* lifetime.

ional sciences; they are in the position of only seeing effects.

Even the points attributed to cause in the physical universe are only treated so in relation to the visible effects and relationships that are observed at the level of continuity making up the physical universe. Just as the "RCC" *Reactive-response Control Center* may be said to be a cause on the physiologic functions and biochemistry of a genetic-body, we can be certain that it is not the definitive cause for all of its activity—but rather a relay station that operates much more closely to the level of manifestation than we deem physical and observable at that level of existence.

Therefore, the "RCC" is approximately the extent to which conventional physical sciences have had any understanding or reality on the human condition. "Stimulus-Response" is about as far as they ever reached in understanding what the being *is*, and yet not one of us who has at least taken a peek behind the curtain a time or two would actually believe that *Self* is nothing more than physical chemical elements charged with a bit of electricity. This is the basic "humans are animals" mentality that has kept the state of the human condition forever trapped amidst the lowest level meanderings.

Keep in mind that the identification of *Self* with the physical is what has gotten the Seeker into their mess in the first place. In fact, we can actually gauge just how "solid" an individual has become simply by taking a look at the *Beta-Awareness Scale*. The lower their attentions are fixed on the scale, the more solid they become. And when the *Self* has identified with a body that is experienced deep levels of depression, apathy and hopelessness... they are quite solid in their existence and they are much more subject to the "impact" of condensed "solid" energies. They are only a few units of *Awareness* away from being at the level of the inert material existence as a genetic being— and as a spiritual being, we have discovered that the Alpha-Spirit can sink into much deeper trappings of consideration than even "body-death."

Barriers imposed in the "Mind" and those extant in the physical universe are all "solid," which is to say, all "things." And as such, "things" and "solids" begin to be treated synonymously with no distinction—and yet we know that there are many levels of manifestation and solidity. As an individual begins to consider only the mechanistic and material basis of their *beta-existence*, the "things" and "solids" are treated by Self as a higher significance or range of evaluation than they actually are. It is the *Awareness* that has been lowered or fixed upon the line, but the "things" are not any more solid at the higher-levels where Self actually *is*.

This issue causes fragmentation, which is simply treating things other than what they actually are. But then we say, well, everyone deserves an opinion and has the ability to makeup the reality and universe that they wish to see things as. And this is, to a great extent, very true. However, we have already placed upon ourselves a condition— or been put in agreements with a condition—that we still are identifying with the lower-level range of experience exhibited by a physical body.

An individual must operate outside the confines and boundaries put in place in order to ensure an actual higher-level cause to a beta-effect. Otherwise we are still operating from within confines of a small cubicle of potential considerations and believing we swim in free expression. It is only free to the extent that barriers have been enforced or designed or agreed to—and while we can be certain that the physical universe and its level of existence is bound by the LAW, the majority of an individual's barriers and imprints and fragmentation are not necessarily due to the LAW imposing some arbitrary punishments. Instead these result from a person not operating in conjunction with the basic energy-matter LAW, and therefore creating and considering more barriers to be in place than there actually are. The barriers are made real, at least to the individual, by acting or reacting on them as terminals —and fragmentation ensues on the line.

Philosophies behind "objective processing" are many—but if nothing else, the methods represent a powerful toolkit to help remedy attentions and increase certainty of an individual in focusing on what they *can* do and the ability of control they *do* have. But there is another reason this is important, because it serves a purpose to resolve another an issue that has been found to come up in most intensive experiments of effective processing; and that is the subject of "loss."

An individual can get a sense that they "lose" something important by giving up a hold on some reactive-response mechanism or mental image or another facet of automatic programming that they have become accustomed to as perhaps even a small basis of fact as reality. Even the dissolution of solids on a communication line or energetic circuit with a terminal can actual generate a great "feeling" of loss; sometimes the individual even feels as though they have just been witness to an explosion. This is one reason why we alternate internalized or subjective work of any kind with "objective processing" as a standard. This should limit the intensity of these occurrences naturally, rather than waiting until after a Seeker has blown off so many charges that they are too confused to bring their attentions back to objects and spaces in their immediate environment.

This information is based on research conducted and discoveries resulting from experimental methods used at the *NexGen Systemology Society* of the *Mardukite Research Organization*. It is provided in hopes that an individual working to be a *Professional Pilot of Systemology* is working toward the betterment of the planet and the elevation of their fellow humans to a higher state of existence known as *Homo Novus*. The work is not perfect, but it represents the best of what we have developed to date—and obviously, given this is *Grade-IV,* the full extent of potential work is not yet completed; yet the journey ahead is well founded—it has been traveled by a select few of now and a few that have gone on before us.

Those who do not adhere to these practices and suggestions will simply find that their own experience of this work is not really "systematic" and open to a lot of setbacks. Those that try to simply plunge through to the uppermost routes of potential work or run nothing but intensive mental exercises to attempt to expedite overt "mental abilities" (while believing that objective processing is a waste of time) &tc.—these individuals will not find balanced stable progression on the *Pathway* and will be likely to be the same individuals that later denounce it.

It is a Pilot's responsibility to make certain that our Systemology continues to effectively grow, be represented appropriately, and through this, always working toward the ideal goals for the spiritual evolution of the human condition—and its highest state of potential knowing and being as the Alpha-Spirit.

METAHUMAN DESTINATIONS

— GLOSSARY —

MARDUKITE SYSTEMOLOGY
CLASS-2C LIBER-TWO EDIT

SYSTEMOLOGY GLOSSARY (v.5.0)

A-for-A (one-to-one) : an expression meaning that what we say, write, represent, think or symbolize is a direct and perfect reflection or duplication of the actual aspect or thing—that "A" is for, means and is equivalent to "A" and not "a" or "q" or "!"; in the relay of communication, the message or particle is sent and perfectly duplicated in form and meaning when received.

aberration : a departure from what is right; in chromatic light science, the failure of a mirror, lens or refracting surface to produce an exact *"one-to-one"* or *"A-for-A"* duplication between an object and its image; a deviation from, or distortion in, what is true or right or straight; in *NexGen Systemology*, a term to describe *fragmentation* as it applies to an individual, which causes them to "stray" form the *Pathway.*

abreaction (abreactive therapy) : the "burn off" or "purging" or "discharge" of "unconscious" (reactive response) as applied to early 20th century German psychology, from *abreagieren*, meaning "coming down" from a release or expression of a repressed or forgotten emotion; in *NexGen Systemology*, fully "resurfacing" traumatic past experiences consciously (on one's own determinism) in order to purge them of their emotional excess (or "charge"); also *"Route-1"* and *"catharsis."*

acid-test : a metaphor refers to a chemical process of applying harsh nitric acid to a golden substance (sample) to determine its genuineness; in *NexGen Systemology*, an extreme conclusive process to determine the reality, genuineness or truth of a substance, material, particle or piece of information.

acknowledgment : a response-communication establishing that an immediately former communication was properly received, duplicated and understood; the formal acceptance and/or recognition of a communication or presence.

activating event : an incident or occurrence that automatically stimulates a conscious or unrecognized reminder or 'ping' from an earlier *imprinting incident* recorded on one's own personal timeline as an emotionally charged and encoded memory; an incident or instance when thought systems are activated to determine the consequence or significance of an activity, motion or event—often demonstrated as *Activating Event → Belief Systems → Consideration.*

actualization : to make actual, not just potential; to bring into full solid Reality; to realize fully in *Awareness* as a "thing."

affinity : the apparent and energetic *relationship* between substances or bodies; the degree of *attraction* or repulsion between things based on natural forces; the *similitude* of frequencies or waveforms; the degree of *interconnection* between systems.

agreement (reality) : unanimity of opinion of what is "thought" to be known; an accepted arrangement of how things are; things we consider as "real" or as an "is" of "reality"; a consensus of what is real as made by standard-issue (common) participants; what an individual contributes to or accepts as "real"; in *NexGen Systemology*, a synonym for "*reality.*"

allegorical : a representation of the abstract, metaphysical or "spiritual" using physical or concrete forms.

alpha : the first, primary, basic, superior or beginning of some form; in *NexGen Systemology*, referring to the state of existence operating on spiritual archetypes and postulates, will and intention "exterior" to the low-level condensation and solidarity of energy and matter as the 'physical universe'.

alpha control center (ACC) : the highest relay point of *Beingness* for an individuated *Alpha-Spirit*, *Self* or "I-AM"; in *NexGen Systemology*—a point of spiritual separation of ZU at (7.0) from the *Infinity of Nothingness* (8.0); the truest actualization of *Identity*; the highest

Self-directed relay of *Alpha-Self* as an *Identity-Continuum*, operating in an *alpha-existence* (or "Spiritual Universe"–AN) to *determine* "Alpha Thought" (6.0) and WILL-*Intention* (5.0) *exterior* to the "Physical Universe"–(KI); the "wave-peak" of "I" emerging as individuated consciousness from *Infinity.*

alpha-spirit : a "spiritual" *Life*-form; the "true" *Self* or I-AM; the *individual*; the spiritual (*alpha*) *Self* that is animating the (*beta*) physical body or *"genetic vehicle"* using a continuous *Lifeline* of spiritual (*"ZU"*) energy; an individual spiritual (*alpha*) entity possessing no physical mass or measurable waveform (motion) in the Physical Universe as itself, so it animates the (*beta*) physical body or *"genetic vehicle"* as a catalyst to experience *Self*-determined causality in effect within the *Physical Universe*; a singular unit or point of *Spiritual Awareness* that is *Aware* that it is *Aware.*

alpha thought : the highest spiritual *Self-determination* over creation and existence exercised by an Alpha-Spirit; the Alpha range of pure *Creative Ability* based on direct postulates and considerations of *Beingness*; spiritual qualities comparable to "thought" but originating in Alpha-existence (at "6.0") independently superior to a *beta-anchored* Mind-System, although an Alpha-Spirit may use Will ("5.0") to carry the intentions of a postulate or consideration ("6.0") to the Master Control Center ("4.0").

amplitude : the quality of being *ample*; the size or amount of energy that is demonstrated in a *wave.* In the case of audio waves, we associate amplitude with "volume." It is not a statement about the frequencies of waves, only how "loud" they are—to what extent they are or may be projected (or audible).

AN : an ancient "Sumerian" cuneiform sign for Heaven or "God"; in *Mardukite Zuism and Systemology* designating the *'spiritual zone'* (or *'Alpha Existence'*); the *Spiritual Universe*—comprised of spiritual matter and spiritual energy; a direction of motion toward spiritual

Infinity, away from or superior to the physical (*'KI'*); the spiritual condition of existence providing for our primary *Alpha* state as an individual *Identity* or *I-AM-Self* which interacts and experiences *Awareness* of a *beta* state in the *Physical Universe* (*'KI'*) as *Life*.

anathema : a thing or person to be detested, loathed or avoided; a thing or person accursed or despised such as to wish damnation or "divine punishment" upon.

anchor (conceptual) : a stable point in space; a fixed point used to hold or stabilize a spatial existence of other points; a spatial point that fixes the parameters of dimensional orientation, such as the corner-points of a solid object in relation to other points in space; in *Nex-Gen Systemology*, "beta-anchored" is an expression used to describe the fixed orientation of a viewpoint from Self in relation to all possible spatial points in *beta-existence* ("physical universe"), or else the existential points that fix the operation of the "body" within the space-time of *beta-existence*.

Ancient Mystery School : the original arcane source of all esoteric knowledge on Earth, concentrated between the Middle East and modern-day Turkey and Transylvania c. 6000 B.C. and then dispersing south (Mesopotamia), west (Europe) and east (Asia) from that location.

antinomian : a term applied to *Gnostics* (popularized by Martin Luther during the Christian reformation) denoting a rejection of formal religious morals and dogma —decreed, written and interpreted by humanity—as a true pathway to Ascension (some elements appear in all forms of religious protest and reformation but as an extreme, would be considered spirto-religious rebellious punkdom by some modern standards, but it should be understood that it does follow a higher ethic, such as Mardukite Utilitarianism.

apotheosis : from the *Greek* word, meaning "*to deify*"; the highest point or apex (for example, of "true knowledge" and "true experience"); an ultimate development of; a glorified or "deified" *ideal*, such as is a quality of *godhood*.

apparent : visibly exposed to sight; evident rather than actual, as presumed by Observation; readily perceived, especially by the senses.

a-priori : from "cause" to "effect"; from a general application to a particular instance; existing in the mind prior to, and independent of experience or observation; validity based on consideration and deduction rather than experience.

archetype : a "first form" or ideal conceptual model of some aspect; the ultimate prototype of a form on which all other conceptions are based.

ascension : actualized *Awareness* elevated to the point of true "spiritual existence" exterior to *beta existence*. An "Ascended Master" is one who has returned to an incarnation on Earth as an inherently *Enlightened One*, demonstrable in their actions—they have the ability to *Self-direct* the "Spirit" as *Self*, just as we are treating the "Mind" and "Body" at this current grade of instruction; previously treated in *Moroii ad Vitam* as a state of Beingness after *First Death*, experienced by an *etheric body*, which is able to maintain consciousness as a personal identity continuum with the same *Self-directed* control and communication of Will-Intention that is exercised, actualized and developed deliberately during one's present incarnation.

assessment scale : an official assignment of graded/gradient numeric values.

associative knowledge : significance or meaning of a facet or aspect assigned to (or considered to have) a direct relationship with another facet; to connect or relate ideas or facets of existence with one another; a reactive-response image, emotion or conception that is suggested by (or directly accompanies) something other than itself; in traditional systems logic, an equivalency of significance or meaning between facets or sets that are grouped together, such as in $(a + b) + c = a + (b + c)$; in Nex-Gen Systemology, erroneous associative knowledge is assignment of the same value to all facets or parts considered as related (even when they are not actually so), such as in $a = a, b = a, c = a$ and so forth without distinction.

assumption : the act of taking or gathering to one's Self; taking possession of, receive or behold.

attenergy : *NexGen Systemological NewSpeak* for "attention energies"; the flow of consciousness "energy" that is directed as "attention"; semantic recognition of an axiom from the *Arcane Tablets* that states: "energy flows where attention goes."

attention : active use of *Awareness* toward a specific aspect or thing; the act of "attending" with the presence of *Self*; a direction of focus or concentration of *Awareness* along a particular channel or conduit or toward a particular terminal node or communication termination point; the Self-directed concentration of personal energy as a combination of observation, thought-waves and consideration; focused application of *Self-Directed Awareness*.

authoritarian : knowledge as truth, boundaries and freedoms dictated to an individual by a perceived, regulated or enforced "authority."

auto-suggestion (self-hypnosis) : auto-conditioning; self-programming; delivering directed affirmations or statements repeatedly to *Self* in order to condition a change in behavior or beliefs; any *Self-directed* technique intended to generate a specific "*post-hypnotic suggestion.*"

awareness : the highest sense of-and-as Self in knowing and being as I-AM (the *Alpha-Spirit*); the extent of beingness directed as a POV experienced by Self as knowingness.

Babylonian : the ancient Mesopotamian civilization

that evolved in the midst of *Sumerian* culture; inception point for systematization of civic society and religion.

band : a division or group; in *NexGen Systemology*, a division or set of frequencies on the ZU-line that are tuned closely together and referred to as a group.

BAT (Beta-Awareness Test) : a method of *psychometric evaluation* developed for *Mardukite Systemology* to determine a "basic" or "average" state of personal *beta-Awareness*; first developed for the text "*Crystal Clear.*"

"bell, book & candle" : three dissimilar objects that are kept accessible during a processing session (the book is often a copy of *The Systemology Handbook* or a hardcover copy of *The Tablets of Destiny* with the dustjacket removed if it is less distracting that way); a term meant to indicate a Pilot's "objective processing kit" of objects generally present in the session room (accessible on a shelf, table or pedestal stands); in *NexGen Systemology,* the name of an objective processing philosophy pertaining to command of personal reality; historically, a formal ritual used by the Roman Catholic church to ceremonially declare an individual "guilty of the most heinous sins" as "excommunicated (to hold no further communications with) by anathema"—whereby a *bell* is rung, a *holy book* is closed and all *candles* are snuffed out—thus we therapeutically use the same symbolism historically representing religious fragmentation for modern systematic defragmentation purposes.

beta (awareness) : all consciousness activity ("*Awareness*") in the "Physical Universe" (KI) or else *beta-existence*; *Awareness* within the range of the *genetic-body*, including material thoughts, emotional responses and physical motors; personal *Awareness* of physical energy and physical matter moving through physical space and experienced as "time"; the *Awareness* held by *Self* that is restricted to a physical organic *Lifeform* or "*genetic vehicle*" in which it experiences causality in the *Physical Universe*.

beta (existence) : all manifestation in the "Physical Universe" (KI); the "Physical" state of existence consisting of vibrations of physical energy and physical matter moving through physical space and experienced as "time"; the conditions of *Awareness* for the *Alpha-spirit* (*Self*) as a physical organic *Lifeform* or "*genetic vehicle*" in which it experiences causality in the *Physical Universe*.

beta-defragmentation : toward a state of *Self-Honesty* in regards to handling experience of the "Physical Universe" (*beta-existence*); an applied spiritual philosophy (or technology) of Self-Actualization originally described in the text "*Crystal Clear*" (*Liber-2B*), building upon theories from "*Systemology: The Original Thesis*."

biological unconsciousness : the organism independent of the sentient *Awareness* of the *Self* to direct it; states induced by severe injury and anesthesia.

biomagnetic/biofeedback : a measurable effect, such as a change in electrical resistance, that is produced by thoughts, emotions and physical behaviors which generate specific 'neurotransmitters' and biochemical reactions in the brain, body and across the skin surface.

cacophony : dissonant, turbulent, harsh and/or discordant sound or noise.

capable : the actual capacity for potential ability.

catalog / catalogue : a systematic list of knowledge or record of data.

catalyst : something that causes action between two systems or aspects, but which itself is unaffected as a variable of this energy communication; a medium or intermediary channel.

catharsis / cathartic processing : from the Greek root meaning "pure" or "perfect"; Gnostic practices of "consolamentum" where an individual removes distorting/fragmented emotional charges and encoding from a personal energy flow/circuit connected or associated with some terminal, mass, thing, *&tc.*; in *NexGen Systemology*, the emptying out or discharge of emotional stores; also *"abreaction"* or *"Route-1."*

causative : as being the cause; to be at cause.

chakra : an archaic Sanskrit term for "wheel" or "spinning circle" used in *Eastern* wisdom traditions, spiritual systems and mysticism; a concept retained in NexGen Systemology to indicate etheric concentrations of energy into wheel-mechanisms that process *ZU* energy at specific frequencies along the *ZU-line*, of which the *Human Condition* is reportedly attached *seven* at various degrees as connected to the Gate symbolism.

channel : a specific stream, course, current, direction or route; to form or cut a groove or ridge or otherwise guide along a specific course; a direct path; an artificial aqueduct created to connect two water bodies or water or make travel possible.

charge : to fill or furnish with a quality; to supply with energy; to lay a command upon; in *NexGen Systemology*—to imbue with intention; to overspread with emotion; application of *Self-directed (WILL)* "intention" toward an emotional manifestation in beta-existence; personal energy stores and significances entwined as fragmentation in mental images, reactive-response encoding and intellectual (and/or) programmed beliefs; in traditional mysticism, to intentionally fix an energetic resonance to meet some degree, or to bring a specific concentration of energy that is transferred to a focal point, such as an object or space.

circuit : a circular path or loop; a closed-path within a system that allows a flow; a pattern or action or wave movement that follows a specific route or potential path only; in *NexGen Systemology*, *"communication processing"* pertaining to a specific flow of energy or information along a channel; *see* also *"feedback loop."*

Circuit-1 : in *Grade-IV* "communication processing" (introduced in *Metahuman Destinations* as *Route-3*), the flow of energy and information connected to outflow, what *Self* has expressed, projected outwardly or done.

Circuit-2 : in *Grade-IV* "communication processing" (introduced in *Metahuman Destinations* as *Route-3*), the flow of energy and information connected to inflow, what "others" have done to *Self*, what it has received inwardly or had *happen to*.

Circuit-3 : in *Grade-IV* "communication processing" (introduced in *Metahuman Destinations* as *Route-3*), the flow of energy and information connected to cross-flows, what *Self* has witnessed of others (or another) projecting or doing toward others (or another).

Circuit-0 : a more advanced concept introduced to *Grade-IV* "communication processing" (as listed on SOP-2C in *Metahuman Destinations* for "*Pre-A.T*" or "*Route-0*" applications), which targets *'postulates'* and *'considerations'* generated and stored by *Self* for *Self* and the direction, energy or flows representing what *Self* "does" for and/or to *Self.* This circuit is treated further in *Wizard Level* work,

chronologically : concerning or pertaining to "time"; to treat as "units" of "time" ; to sequence a series of events or information with regard to the order it happened or originated (in time).

clockwork : rigidly fixed gear-like systems that operate mechanically and directly upon one another to function; a "clockwork universe theory" is a "closed-system design" popular in Newtonian Physics attributes all actions of energy-matter in space-time as reactions in accordance with a "Divine Decree" or fixed design that functions like a "clock-mechanism" and does not account for the "Observer."

codification : process of collecting, analyzing and then arranging knowledge in a standardized and more accessible systematic form, often by subject, theme or some other designation.

collapsing a wave : also, *"wave-function collapse"*; in *Quantum Physics*, the concept that an Observer is "collapsing" the wave-function to something "definite" by measuring it; defining or calculating a wave-function or interaction of potential interactions by an Observation; in *NexGen Systemology*, when a wave of potentiality or possibility because a finite fixed form; Consciousness or *Awareness* "collapses" a wave-function of energy-matter as a necessary "third" Principle of Apparent Manifestation (first described in *"Tablets of Destiny"*); potentiality as a wave is collapsed into an apparent *"is"*, the energy of which is freed up in systematic processing by *"flattening"* a "collapsed" wave back into its state of potentiality.

command : in *Metahuman Systemology*, responsibility and ability of Self (I-AM) as operating from its ideal "exterior" *Point-of-View* as Alpha Spirit; to direct communication for control of the *genetic vehicle* and Mind-Body connection that is perfectly duplicated from a source-point to a receipt-point along the ZU-line.

command line : see *"processing command line"* (PCL).

common knowledge (game theory) : facts that all "players" know, and they know that all other "players" also know—such as the very structure of the "game" being played.

communication : successful transmission of information, data, energy (&tc.) along a message line, with a reception of feedback; an energetic flow of intention to cause an effect (or duplication) at a distance; the personal energy moved or acted upon by will or else 'selective directed attention'; the 'messenger action' used to transmit and receive energy across a medium; also relay of energy, a message or signal—or even locating a personal POV (viewpoint) for the Self—along the *ZU-line*.

communication (circuit) processing : a methodology of Grade-IV Metahuman Systemology that emphasizes analysis of all Mind-System energy flows (information) transmitted and stored along circuits of a channel toward some terminal, thing or concept, particularly: what Self has out-flowed, what Self has in-flowed, and the cross-flows that Self has observed; also *"Route-3"*

compulsion : a failure to be responsible for the dynamics of control—starting, stopping or altering—on a particular channel of communication and/or regarding a particular terminal in existence; an energetic flow with the appearance of being 'stuck' on the action it is already doing or by the control of some automatic mechanism.

computing device : a calculator or modern computer; a mechanism that performs specific functions, particularly input, output and storage of data/information.

condense (condensation) : the transition of vapor to liquid; denoting a change in state to a more substantial or solid condition; leading to a more compact or solid form.

condition : an apparent or existing state; circumstances, situations and variable dynamics affecting the order and function of a system; a series of interconnected requirements, barriers and allowances that must be met; in "contemporary language," bringing a thing toward a specific, desired or intentional new state (such as in "conditioning"), though to minimize confusion about the word "condition" in our literature, *NexGen Systemology* treats "contemporary conditioning" concepts as imprinting, encoding and programming.

conflict : the opposition of two forces of similar magnitude along the same channel or competing for the same terminal; the inability to duplicate another POV; a thought, intention or communication that is met with an opposing counter-thought or counter-intention that generates an energetic cluster.

confront : to come around in front of; to be in the presence of; to stand in front of, or in the face of; to meet "face-to-face" or "face-up-to"; additionally, in *NexGen Systemology*, to fully tolerate or acceptably withstand an encounter with a particular manifestation or encounter.

consciousness : the energetic flow of *Awareness*; the Principle System of *Awareness* that is spiritual in nature, which demonstrates potential interaction with all degrees of the Physical Universe; the *Beingness* component of our existence in *Spirit*; the Principle System of *Awareness* as *Spirit* that directs action in the Mind-System.

consensual (consensus) : formed or existing simply by consent—by general or mutual agreement; permitted, approved or agreed upon by majority of opinion; knowingly agreed upon unanimously by all concerned; to be in agreement on the objective universe and/or a course of action therein.

consideration : careful analytical reflection of all aspects; deliberation; determining the significance of a "thing" in relation to similarity or dissimilarity to other "things"; evaluation of facts and importance of certain facts; thorough examination of all aspects related to, or important for, making a decision; the analysis of consequences and estimation of significance when making decisions; in *NexGen Systemology*, the postulate or Alpha-Thought that defines the state of beingness for what something "*is.*"

continuity : being a continuous whole; a complete whole or "total round of"; the balance of the equation ["–120" + "120" = "0" *&tc.*]; an apparent unbroken interconnected coherent whole; also, as applied to Universes in *NexGen Systemology*, the lowest base consideration of space-time or commonly shared level of energy-matter apparent in an existence, or else the lowest degree of solidity or condensation whereby all mass that exists is identifiable or communicable with all other mass that exists; represented as "0" on the *Standard Model* for the Physical Universe (*beta-existence*), a level of existence that is below Human emotion, comparable to the solidity of "rocks" and "walls" and "inert bodies."

continuum : a continuous enduring uninterrupted sequence or condition; observing all gradients on a *spectrum*; measuring quantitative variation with gradual transition on a spectrum without demonstrating discontinuity or separate parts.

control (systems) : Communication relayed from an operative center or organizational cluster, which incites new activity elsewhere in a system (or along the *ZU-line*).

correlate : a relationship between two or more aspects, parts or systems.

correspondence : a direct relationship or correlation; see also *"associative knowledge."*

Cosmic History : the entire continuous *Spiritual Timeline* of all existence, starting with the *Infinity of Nothingness* and individuation of Self and its Home Universe, running through various Games Universes and ultimately leading to condensation and solidification of this Physical Universe experienced in present-time.

Cosmic Law : the "Law" of Nature (or the Physical Universe); the "Law" governing cosmic ordering; often called "Natural Law" in sciences and philosophies that attempt to codify or systematize it.

cosmology : a systematic philosophy defining origins and structure of an apparent Universe.

Cosmos : archaic term for the "Physical Universe"; semantically implies chaos brought into order; in *NexGen Systemology*, can also include considerations of "Universes" experienced previously as a *beta-existence*.

counter-productive : contrary to the greater or original purpose or intention; in *NexGen Systemology*, anything which brings *Life* away from its sustainable goal or position of *Infinite Existence*.

crash-coursed : a very intense or steep delivery of education over a very brief time period, usually applied to bring a student "up-to-speed" or "up-to-date" for receiving and understanding newer or cumulatively more advanced material.

Crossing the Abyss : to enter the spiritual or metaphysical unknown in "Self-annihilation" to purify the Self and "return to the Source."

Crystal Clear : the second professional publication of Mardukite Systemology, released publicly in December 2019; the second professional text in Grade-III Mardukite Systemology, released as "*Liber-2B*" and reissued in the Grade-III Master Edition "*Systemology Handbook*"; contains fundamental theory of "*Beta-Defragmentation*" and "*Route-2*" systematic processing methodology.

cuneiform : the oldest extant writing system at the inception of modern civilization in Mesopotamia; a system of wedge-shaped script inscribed on clay tablets with a reed pen, allowing advancements in record keeping and communication no longer restricted to more literal graphic representations or pictures.

cuneiform signs : the cuneiform script, as used in ancient Mesopotamia, is not represented in a linear alphabet of "letters," but by a systematic use of basic word "signs" that are combined to form more complex word "signs"—each sign represented a "sound" more than it did a letter, such as "ab," "ad", "ba", "da" *&tc*.

data-set : the total accumulation of knowledge used to base Reality.

dead-memories : outdated, inadequate or erroneous data.

defragmentation : the *reparation* of wholeness; collecting all dispersed parts to reform an original whole; a process of removing "*fragmentation*" in data or knowledge to provide a clear understanding; applying techniques and processes that promote a *holistic* interconnected *alpha* state, favoring observational

Awareness of continuity in all spiritual and physical systems; in *NexGen Systemology*, a *"Seeker"* achieving an actualized state of basic *"Self-Honest Awareness"* is said to be *beta-defragmented*, whereas *Alpha-defragmentation* is the rehabilitation of the *creative ability*, managing the *Spiritual Timeline* and the POV of *Self* as Alpha-Spirit (I-AM); see also *"Beta-defragmentation."*

degree : a physical or conceptual *unit* (or point) defining the variation present relative to a *scale* above and below it; any stage or extent to which something *is* in relation to other possible positions within a *set* of *"parameters"*; a point within a specific range or spectrum; in *NexGen Systemology*, a *Seeker's* potential energy variations or fluctuations in thought, emotional reaction and physical perception are all treated as *"degrees."*

demographics : segments of the population uniquely identified, whether real or representative; targeting a specific portion of the population, such as for marketing or statistics.

destiny : what is set down, made firm, standard, or stands fixed as a constant end; the absolute *destination* regardless of whatever course is traveled; in *NexGen Systemology*, the *"destiny"* of the *"Human Spirit"* (or *"Alpha Spirit"*) is infinite existence—*"Immortality."*

dichotomy : a division into two parts, types or kinds.

differential : the quantitative value difference between two forces, motions, pressures or degrees.

differentiation : an apparent difference between aspects or concepts.

discernment : to perceive, distinguish and/or differentiate experience into true knowledge.

displace : to compel to leave; to move or replace something with something else in its place or space.

dissonance : discordance; out of step; out of phase; disharmonious; the "differential" between the way things are and the way things are experienced; cognitive dissonance could be demonstrated as A = abc, or C = A, the duplication of truth/communication is not A-for-A.

dross : prime material; specifically waste-matter or refuse; the discarded remains collected together.

dynamic (systems) : a principle or fixed system which demonstrates its *'variations'* in activity (or output) only in constant relation to variables or fluctuation of interrelated systems; a standard principle, function, process or system that exhibits *'variations'* and change simultaneously with all connected systems; each *'Sphere of Existence'* is a dynamic system, systematically affecting (supporting) and affected (supported) by other *'Spheres'* (which are also dynamic systems).

Eastern traditions : the evolution of the *Ancient Mystery School* east of its origins, primarily the Asian continent, or what is archaically referred to as "oriental."

echelon : a level or rung on a ladder; a rank or level of command.

eclipse : to cast a shadow or darken; to block out or obscure a comparison.

elocution : the skillful use of clearly directed and expressive speech; the expert demonstration of articulation, pronunciation and dictation to express a message.

emotional encoding : the readable substance/material (data) of *'imprints'*; associations of sensory experience with an *imprint*; perceptions of our environment that receive an *emotional charge*, which form or reinforce facets of an *imprint*; perceptions recorded and stored as an *imprint* within the "emotional range" of energetic manifestation; the formation of an energetic store or charge on a channel that fixes emotional responses as a mechanistic automation, which is carried on in an individual's *Spiritual Timeline* (or personal continuum of existence).

enact : to make happen; to bring into action; to make part of an act.

encompassing : to form a circle around, surround or envelop around.

end point : the moment when the goal of a process has been achieved and to continue on with it will be detrimental to the gains; the finality of a process when the *Seeker* has achieved their optimum state from the current cycle (whether or not they run through it again at a later date with a different level of *Awareness* or knowledge base doesn't change the fact that it has flattened the standing wave

energetic exchange : communicated transmission of energetically encoded "information" between fields, forces or source-points that share some degree of interconnectivity; the event of "waves" acting upon each other like a force, flowing in regard to their proximity, range, frequency and amplitude.

energy signatures : a distinctive pattern of energetic action.

enforcement : the act of compelling or putting (effort) into force; to compel or impose obedience by force; to impress strongly with applications of stress to demand agreement or validation; the lowest-level of direct control by physical effort or threat of punishment; a low-level method of control in the absence of true communication.

engineering : the *Self-directed* actions and efforts to utilize knowledge (observed causality/science), maths (calculations/quantification) and logic (axioms/formulas) to understand, design or manifest a solid structure, machine, mechanism, engine or system; as *"Reality Engineering"* in *NexGen Systemology*—intentional *Self-directed* adjustment of existing Reality conditions; the application of total *Self-determinism* in *Self-Honesty* to change apparent Reality using fundamentals of *System-ology* and *Cosmic Law*.

entanglement : tangled together; intertwined and en-meshed systems; in *NexGen Systemology*, a reference to the interrelation of all particles as waves at a higher point of connectivity than is apparent, since wave-func-tions only "collapse" when someone is *Observing*, or doing the measuring, evaluating, &tc.

entropy : the reduction of organized physical systems back into chaos-continuity when their integrity is meas-ured against space over time; reduction toward a zero-point.

epicenter : the point from which shock-waves travel.

epistemology : a school of philosophy focused on the truth of knowledge and knowledge of truth; theories re-garding validity and truth inherent in any structure of knowledge and reason; the original "school of philo-sophy" from which all other "disciplines" were derived; the study of knowing how to know knowledge, reason and truth.

erroneous : inaccurate; incorrect; containing error.

esoteric : hidden; secret; knowledge understood by a se-lect few.

etching : to cut, bite or corrode with acid to produce a pattern.

evaluate : to determine, assign or fix a set value, amount or meaning.

exacting : a demanding rigid effort to draw forth from.

executable : the supreme authoritative ability to carry out according to design.

existence : the *state* or fact of *apparent manifestation*; the resulting combination of the Principles of Manifesta-tion: consciousness, motion and substance; continued *survival*; that which independently exists; the *'Prime Directive'* and sole purpose of all manifestation or Reality; the highest common intended motivation driving any *"Thing"* or *Life*.

existential : pertaining to existence, or some aspect or condition of existence.

exoteric : public knowledge or common understanding; the level of understanding and *Knowing* maintained by the "masses"; how a thing is generally understood "by all" or the opposite of *esoteric*.

experiential data : accumulated reference points we store as memory concerning our "experience" with Reality.

extant : in existence; existing.

extrapolate : to make an estimate of the "value" outside of the perceivable range.

extropy : *NexGen Systemology NewSpeak*—the reduction of organized spiritual systems back into a singularity of Infinity when their integrity is measured against space over time; reduction toward an infinitude; the opposite of *entropy*.

facets : an aspect, an apparent phase; one of many faces of something; a cut surface on a gem or crystal; in *Nex-Gen Systemology*—a single perception or aspect of a memory or *"Imprint"*; any one of many ways in which a memory is recorded; perceptions associated with a painful emotional (sensation) experience and *"imprinted"* onto a metaphoric lens through which to view future similar experiences; other secondary terminals that are associated with a particular terminal, painful event or experience of loss, and which may exhibit the same encoded significance as the activating event.

faculties : abilities of the mind (individual) inherent or developed.

fallacy : a deceptive, misleading, erroneous and/or false beliefs; unsound logic; persuasions, invalidation or enforcement of Reality agreements based on authority, sympathy, bandwagon/mob mentality, vanity, ambiguity, suppression of information, and/or presentation of false dichotomies.

fate : what is brought to light or actualized as experi-ence; the actual *course* taken to reach an end, charted end, or final *destination*; in *NexGen Systemology*, the *'fate'* of a *'Human Spirit'* (or *'Alpha Spirit'*) is determ-ined by the choice of course taken to experience *Life.*

feedback loop : a complete and continuous circuit flow of energy or information directed as an output from a source to a target which is altered and return back to the source as an input; in *General Systemology*—the con-tinuous process where outputs of a system are routed back as inputs to complete a circuit or loop, which may be closed or connected to other systems/circuits; in *Nex-Gen Systemology*—the continuous process where directed *Life* energy and *Awareness* is sent back to *Self* as experience, understanding and memory to complete an energetic circuit as a loop.

flattening a wave : see *"process-out"* for definition; also see *"collapsing a wave."*

flow : movement across (or through) a channel (or con-duit); a direction of active energetic motion typically distinguished as either an *in-flow, out-flow* or *cross-flow.*

fractal : a wave-curve, geometric figure, form or pat-tern, with each part representative of the same characteristics as the whole; any baseline, sequence or pattern where the 'whole' is found in the 'parts' and the 'parts' contain the 'whole'; a pattern that reoccurs simil-arly at various scales/levels on a continuous whole; a subset of a Euclidean space explored in higher-level academic mathematics, in which fractal dimensions are found to exceed topological ones; in NexGen Systemo-logy, a "fractal-like" description is used specifically for a pattern or form that has a reoccurring nature without regard to what level or scale it is manifest upon. Ex-amples include the formation of crystals, tree-like patterns, the comparison of atoms to solar systems to galaxies, &tc.

fragmentation : breaking into parts and scattering the pieces; the *fractioning* of wholeness or the *fracture* of a holistic interconnected *alpha* state, favoring observational *Awareness* of perceived connectivity between parts; *discontinuity*; separation of a totality into parts; in *NexGen Systemology*, a person outside a state of *Self-Honesty* is said to be *fragmented*.

game : a strategic situation where a "player's" power of choice is employed or affected; a parameter or condition defined by purposes, freedoms and barriers (rules).

game theory : a mathematical theory of logic pertaining to strategies of maximizing gains and minimizing loses within prescribed boundaries and freedoms; a field of knowledge widely applied to human problem solving and decision-making; the application of true knowledge and logic to deduce the correct course of action given all variables and interplay of dynamic systems; logical study of decision making where "players" make choices that affect (the interests) of other "players"; an intellectual study of conflict and cooperation.

general systemology ("systematology") : a methodology of analysis and evaluation regarding the systems—their design and function; organizing systems of interrelated information-processing in order to perform a given function or pattern of functions.

genetic memory : the evolutionary, cellular and genetic (DNA) "memory" encoded into a *genetic vehicle* or *living organism* during its progression and duplication (reproduction) over millions (or billions) of years on Earth; in *NexGen Systemology*—the past-life Earth-memory carried in the genetic makeup of an organism (*genetic vehicle*) that is *independent of any* actual "spiritual memory" maintained by the *Alpha Spirit* themselves, from its own previous lifetimes on Earth and elsewhere using other *genetic vehicles* with no direct evolutionary connection to the current physical form in use.

genetic-vehicle : a physical *Life*-form; the physical (*beta*) body that is animated/controlled by the (*Alpha*) *Spirit* using a continuous *Lifeline* (ZU); a physical (*beta*) organic receptacle and catalyst for the (*Alpha*) *Self* to operate "causes" and experience "effects" within the *Physical Universe*.

gifted : attributing a special quality or ability; having exceptionally high intelligence or mental faculties.

gnosis : a *Greek* word meaning knowledge, but specific-ally "true knowledge"; the highest echelon of "true knowledge" accessible (or attained) only by mystical or spiritual faculties whereby actualized realizations are achieved independent of specialized education.

Gnostics : a name meaning "having knowledge" in Greek language (see also *gnosis*); an early sect of Judeo-Christian mysticism from the 1st Century AD emphasiz-ing true knowledge by *Self-Honest* experience of metahuman and spiritual states of beingness, emphasiz-ing defragmentation of "illusion" and overcoming of material "deception"; an esoteric proto-Systemology or-ganization disbanded by the Roman Church as heretical.

godhood : a divine character or condition; "divinity."

gradient : a degree of partitioned ascent or descent along some scale, elevation or incline; "higher" and "lower" values in relation to one another.

help : to assist survival of; aid continuing optimum suc-cess.

heralded : proclaimed ahead of or prior to; officially announced.

holistic : the examination of interconnected systems as encompassing something greater than the *sum* of their "parts."

Homo Novus : literally, the "new man"; the "newly el-evated man" or "known man" in ancient Rome; the man who "knows (only) through himself"; in NexGen Systemology—the next spiritual and intellectual evolution of *homo sapiens* (the "modern Human Condition"), which is signified by a demonstration of higher faculties of *Self-Actualization* and clear *Awareness*.

Homo Sapiens Sapiens : the present standard-issue Human Condition; the *hominid* species and genetic-line on Earth that received modification, programming and conditioning by the *Anunnaki* race of *Alpha-Spirits*, of which early alterations contributed to various upgrades (changes) to the genetic-line, beginning approximately 450,000 years ago (*ya*) when the *Anunnaki* first appear on Earth; a species for the Human Condition on Earth that resulted from many specific *Anunnaki* "genetic" and "cultural" *interventions* at certain points of significant advancement—specifically (but not limited to) *circa* 300,000 *ya*, 200,000 *ya*, 40,000 *ya*, and 8,000 *ya*; a species of the Human Condition set for replacement by *Homo Novus*.

hot button : something that triggers or incites an intense emotional reaction instantaneously; in *NexGen Systemology*—a slang term denoting a highly reactive *channel*, heavily *charged* with a long chain of cumulative *emotional imprinting*, typically (but not necessarily) connected to a significant or "primary" *implant*; a non-technical label, first applied during *Grade-IV Professional Piloting "Flight School"* research sessions of Spring-Summer 2020, to indicate specific circuits, channels or terminals that cause a *Seeker* to immediately react with intense emotional responses, whether in general, directed to the *Pilot*, or even at effectiveness of processing.

Human Condition : a standard default state of Human experience that is generally accepted to be the extent of its potential identity (*beingness*)—currently treated as *Homo Sapiens Sapiens,* but which is scheduled for replacement by *Homo Novus*.

humanistic psychology : a field of academic psychology approaching a holistic emphasis on *Self-Actualization* as an individual's most basic motivation; early key figures from the 20th century include: Carl Rogers, Abraham Maslow, L. Ron Hubbard, William Walker Atkinson, Deepak Chopra and Timothy Leary (to name a few).

hypothetical : operating under the assumption a certain aspect actual "is."

identification : the association of *identity* to a thing; a label or fixed data-set associated to what a thing is; association "equals" a thing, the "equals" being key; an equality of all things in a group, for example, an "apple" identified with all other "apples"; the reduction of "I-AM"-*Self* from a *Spiritual Beingness* to an "identity" of some form.

identity : the collection of energy and matter—including memory—across a "*Spiritual Timeline*" that we consider as "I" of *Self*, but the "I" is an individual and not an identification with anything other than *Self* as *Alpha-Spirit*.

identity-system : the application of the *ZU-line* as "I"— the continuous expression of *Self* as *Awareness* across a "*Spiritual Timeline*"; see "*identity*."

illuminated : to supply with light so as to make visible or comprehensible.

imagination : the ability to create *mental imagery* in one's Personal Universe at will and change or alter it as desired; the ability to create, change and dissolve mental images on command or as an act of will; to create a mental image or have associated imagery displayed (or "conjured") in the mind that may or may not be treated as real (or memory recall) and may or may not accurately duplicate objective reality; to employ *Creative Abilities* of the Spirit that are independent of reality agreements with beta-existence.

immersion : plunged (sunk into); wholly surrounded by.

imperative : a high-level authoritarian command; a command triggering urgency and necessity of a certain goal or directive; see also "*Spheres of Existence*" and "*Prime Directive.*"

implant : to graft or surgically insert; to establish firmly by setting into; to instill or install a direct command or consideration in consciousness (Mind-System, &tc.); a mechanical device inserted beneath the surface/skin; in *Metahuman Systemology*, an "energetic mechanism" (linked to an Alpha-Spirit) composing a circuit-network and systematic array of energetic receptors underlying and filter-screening communication channels between the Mind-System and *Self*; an energetic construct in-stalled upon entry of a Universe; similar to a platen or matrix or circuit-board, where each part records a spe-cific type or quality of *emotionally encoded imprints* and other "heavily charged" *Mental Images* that are "impressed" by future encounters; a basic platform on which certain *imprints* and *Mental Images* are encoded (keyed-in) and stored (often beneath the surface of "knowing" or *Awareness* for that individual, although an implanted "command" toward certain inclinations or be-havioral tendencies may be visibly observable.

imprint : to strongly impress, stamp, mark (or outline) onto a softer 'impressible' substance; to mark with pres-sure onto a surface; in *NexGen Systemology*, the term is used to indicate permanent Reality impressions marked by frequencies, energies or interactions experienced dur-ing periods of emotional distress, pain, unconsciousness, loss, enforcement, or something antagonistic to physical (personal) survival, all of which are are stored with oth-er reactive response-mechanisms at lower-levels of *Awareness* as opposed to the active memory database and proactive processing center of the Mind; an experi-ential "memory-set" that may later resurface—be triggered or stimulated artificially—as Reality, of which similar responses will be engaged automatically; holo-graphic-like imagery "stamped" onto consciousness as composed of energetic *facets* tied to the "snap-shot" of an experience.

imprinting incident : the first or original event instance communicated and *emotionally encoded* onto an individual's "*Spiritual Timeline*" (recorded memory from all lifetimes), which formed a permanent impression that is later used to mechanistically treat future contact on that channel; the first or original occurrence of some particular *facet* or mental image related to a certain type of *encoded response*, such as pain and discomfort, losses and victimization, and even the acts that we have taken against others along the Spiritual Timeline of our existence that caused them to also be *Imprinted*.

incarnation : a present, living or concrete form of some thing, idea or beingness; an individual lifetime or lifecycle from birth/creation to death/destruction independent of other lifetimes or cycles.

inception : the beginning, start, origin or outset.

incite : to urge on or cause; instigate; prove or stimulate into action.

indefinable : without a clear definition being currently presented.

individual : a person, lifeform, human entity or creature; a *Seeker* or potential *Seeker* is often referred to as an "individual" within Mardukite Zuism and Systemology materials.

infinite existence : "immortality."

infinitude : being infinite; quantity or quality of *Infinity*.

inhibited : withheld, held-back, discouraged or repressed from some state.

"in phase" : see "*phase alignment.*"

insistence : repeated use of a communicated energy into a form that demands acknowledgment, is more difficult to avoid or ignore.

institution : a social standard or organizational group

responsible for promoting some system or aspect in society.

intention : the directed application of Will; to intend (have "in Mind") or signify (give "significance" to) for or toward a particular purpose; in *NexGen Systemology* (from the *Standard Model*)—the spiritual activity at WILL (5.0) directed by an *Alpha Spirit* (7.0); the application of WILL as "Cause" from a higher order of Alpha Thought and consideration (6.0), which then may continue to relay communications as an "effect" in the universe.

inter-dimensional : systems that are interconnected or correlated between the Physical Universe and the Spiritual Universe—or between "dimension states" observably identified as "physical," "emotional," "psychological" and "spiritual." The only point of true interconnectivity that we can systematically determine is called *"Life"* or the POV of *Self.*

intermediate : a distinct point between two points; actions between two points.

invalidate : decrease the level or degree or *agreement* as Reality.

invest : spend on; give or devote something in exchange for a beneficial result; to endow with.

"kNow" : a creative spelling and use of semantics for *"know"* and *"now"* to indicate the state of present-time actualized "Awareness" as Self (Alpha-Spirit), developed for fun dual-meaning messages made by early Mardukite Systemologists in 2008-9, such as "Live in the kNow" or "Be in the kNow"—and even "Drown in the kNow" (parodying a song featuring Matisyahu, by electronic music duo, *Crystal Method*).

knowledge : clear personal processing of informed understanding; information (data) that is actualized as effectively workable understanding; a demonstrable understanding on which we may 'set' our *Awareness*—or literally a "know-ledge" ("ledge of knowing").

KI : an ancient cuneiform sign designating the *'physical zone'*; the *Physical Universe*—comprised of physical matter and physical energy in action across space and observed as time; a direction of motion toward material *Continuity*, away from or subordinate to the Spiritual (*'AN'*); the physical condition of existence providing for our *beta* state of *Awareness* experienced (and interacted with) as an individual *Lifeform* from our primary Alpha state of Identity or *I-AM-Self* in the *Spiritual Universe* (*'AN'*).

kinetic : pertaining to the energy of physical motion and movement.

learned : highly educated; possessing significant know-ledge.

level : a physical or conceptual *tier* (or plane) relative to a *scale* above and below it; a significant *gradient* observable as a *foundation* (or surface) built upon and subsequent to other levels of a totality or whole; a *set* of *"parameters"* with respect to other such *sets* along a *continuum*; in *NexGen Systemology*, a *Seeker's* understanding, *Awareness* as *Self* and the formal grades of material/instruction are all treated as *"levels."*

Liber-One : First published in October 2019 as *"The Tablets of Destiny: Using Ancient Wisdom to Unlock Human Potential"* by Joshua Free; republished in the complete *Grade-III* anthology, *"The Systemology Handbook"*; revised in August 2022 as *"The Tablets of Destiny (Revelation): How Long-Lost Anunnaki Wisdom Can Change the Fate of Humanity."*

Liber-Two : First published in October 2020 as *"Metahuman Destinations: Piloting the Course to Homo Novus"* by Joshua Free; an anthology of the *Grade-IV* "Professional Piloting Course," containing revised materials from *Liber-2C*, *Liber-2D* and (most of) *Liber-3C*; republished in the complete *Grade-IV* anthology, *"The Metahuman Systemology Handbook."*

Liber-Three : see *"Liber-3E."*

Liber-2B : First published in December 2019 as *"Crystal Clear: The Self-Actualization Manual & Guide to Total Awareness"* by Joshua Free; republished in the complete *Grade-III* anthology, *"The Systemology Handbook"*; revised in April 2022 as *"Crystal Clear (Handbook for Seekers): Achieve Self-Actualization and Spiritual Ascension in This Lifetime."*

Liber-2C : First published in April 2020 as *"Communication and Control of Energy & Power: The Magic of Will & Intention (Volume One)"* by Joshua Free; revision republished as an integral part of the *Grade-IV* "Professional Piloting Course," in October 2020 within *"Metahuman Destinations"* (*Liber-Two*); republished in the complete *Grade-IV* anthology, *"The Metahuman Systemology Handbook."*

Liber-2D : First published in June 2020 as *"Command of the Mind-Body Connection: The Magic of Will & Intention" (Volume Two)"* by Joshua Free; revision republished as an integral part of the *Grade-IV* "Professional Piloting Course," in October 2020 within *"Metahuman Destinations"* (*Liber-Two*); republished in the complete *Grade-IV* anthology, *"The Metahuman Systemology Handbook."*

Liber-3C : First published in July 2020 as *"Now You Know: The Truth About Universes & How You Got Stuck in One"* by Joshua Free; a discourse in the *Grade-IV* Metahuman Systemology series; a revision of one part republished in October 2020 within the *"Professional Piloting Course"* manual, *"Metahuman Destinations"* (*Liber-Two*), a revision of the remaining part republished in June 2021 within the *"Imaginomicon"* (*Liber-3D*); republished in the complete *Grade-IV* anthology, *"The Metahuman Systemology Handbook."*

Liber-3D : First published in June 2021 as *"Imaginomicon: The Gateway to Higher Universes (A Grimoire for the Human Spirit)"* by Joshua Free; a manual completing the *Grade-IV* (Metahuman Systemology) professional series with a treatment of "Wizard Level-0"; revised in June 2022 as *"Imaginomicon (Revised Edition): Approaching Gateways to Higher Universes (A New Grimoire for the Human Spirit)"*; republished in the complete *Grade-IV* anthology, *"The Metahuman Systemology Handbook."*

Liber-3E (Liber-Three) : First published in April 2022 as *"The Way of the Wizard: Utilitarian Systemology (A New Metahuman Ethic)"* by Joshua Free; a professional manual bridging *Grade-IV* (Metahuman Systemology, Wizard Level-0) with *Grade-V* (Spiritual Systemology, Wizard Level-1); republished in the complete *Grade-IV* anthology, *"The Metahuman Systemology Handbook."*

localized : brought together and confined to a particular place.

logic : philosophical science of correct *reasoning*.

logic equations : using symbols and basic mathematical logic to establish the validity of statements or to see how a variable within a system will change the result; a basic demonstration of proportion or relationship between variables in a system.

logistics : pertaining to the movement or transportation between locations.

macrocosmic : taking examples and system demonstrations at one level and applying them as a larger demonstration of a relatively higher level or unseen dimension.

manifestation : something brought into existence.

Marduk : founder of Babylonia; patron Anunnaki "god" of Babylon.

Mardukite Zuism : a Mesopotamian-themed (Babylonian-oriented) religious philosophy and tradition applying the spiritual technology based on *Arcane Tablets* in combination with "Tech" from *NexGen Systemology*; first developed in the New Age underground by Joshua Free in 2008 and realized publicly in 2009 with the formal establishment of the *Mardukite Chamberlains*. The text *"Tablets of Destiny"* is a crossover from Mardukite Zuism (and Mesopotamian Neopaganism) toward higher spiritual applications of Systemology.

Master-Control-Center (MCC) : a perfect computing device to the extent of the information received from "lower levels" of sensory experience/perception; the proactive communication system of the *"Mind"*; a relay point of active *Awareness* along the Identity's *ZU-line*, which is responsible for maintaining basic *Self-Honest Clarity* of *Knowingness* as a *seat of consciousness* between the *Alpha-Spirit* and the secondary *"Reactive Control Center"* of a *Lifeform* in *beta existence*; the Mind-center for an *Alpha-Spirit* to actualize cause in the *beta existence*; the analytical *Self-Determined* Mind-center of an *Alpha-Spirit used* to project *Will* toward the genetic body; the point of contact between *Spiritual Systems* and the *beta existence*; presumably the *"Third Eye"* of a being connected directly to the *I-AM-Self*, which is responsible for *determining* Reality at any time; in *NexGen Systemology*, this is plotted at (4.0) on the continuity model of the *ZU-line*.

"Master Grades" : literary materials by Joshua Free (written between 1995 and 2019) revised and compiled for the "Mardukite Academy of Systemology" instructional grades—"Route of Magick & Mysticism" (*Grade I, Part A*), "Route of Druidism & Dragon Legacy" (*Grade I, Part D*), "Route of Mesopotamian Mysteries" (Grade II) and "Route of Mardukite Systemology" or "Pathway to Self-Honesty" (*Grade III*).

MCC : see *"Master-Control-Center."*

mental image : a subjectively experienced "picture" created and imagined into being by the Alpha-Spirit (or at lower levels, one of its automated mechanisms) that includes all perceptible *facets* of totally immersive scene, which may be forms originated by an individual, or a "facsimile-copy" ("snap-shot") of something seen or encountered; a duplication of wave-forms in one's Personal Universe as a "picture" that mirror an "external" Universe experience, such as an *Imprint*.

Mesopotamia : land between Tigris and Euphrates River; modern-day Iraq; the primary setting for ancient *Sumerian* and *Babylonian* traditions thousands of years ago, including activities and records of the *Anunnaki.*

metahumanism : an applied philosophy of *transhumanism* with an emphasis on "spiritual technologies" as opposed to "external" ones; a new state or evolution of the *Human Condition* achievable on planet Earth, rooted in *Self-Honesty*, whereby individuals are operating *exterior* to considerations that are fixed exclusively to the *genetic vehicle* (Human Body) and independent of the *emotional encoding* and *associative programming* typical of the present standard-issue *Human Condition.*

Metahuman Destinations : the third professional publication of Mardukite Systemology, released publicly in October 2020; the first professional text in Grade-IV Metahuman Systemology, released as "*Liber-Two*" and containing materials from *Liber-2C, Liber-2D* and *Liber-3C*; contains fundamental theory of "*Professional Piloting*" and "*Route-3*" systematic processing methodology.

methodology : a complete system of applications, methods, principles and rules to compose a *'systematic'* paradigm as a "whole"—esp. a field of philosophy or science.

"mind's eye" : following semantics of archaic esoterica, the point where "mental pictures" (and senses) are generated that define what an individual believes they are experiencing in present time; activities or phenomenon described in archaic esoterica as the "Third-Eye" (or actualized MCC) where the *Alpha-Spirit* directly interacts with the organic *genetic vehicle* in *beta-existence*; in the semantics of basic Mardukite Zuism and Hermetic Philosophy, *Self-directed* activity on the plane of "mental consciousness" between "spiritual consciousness" of the *Alpha-Spirit* and "physical/emotional consciousness" of the *genetic vehicle*; *NexGen* 'slang' used to describe "consciousness activity" *Self-directed* by an actualized WILL.

misappropriated : put into use incorrectly; to apply ineffectively or as unintended by design or definition.

motor functions : internal mechanisms that allow a body to move.

Nabu : the *Anunnaki* "god of wisdom, writing and knowledge" for Babylonian (Mardukite) Tradition.

negligible : so small or trifle that it may be disregarded.

neurotransmitter : a chemical substance released at a physiological level (of the genetic vehicle) that bridges communication of energetic transmission between the *Mind-Body* systems, using the "nervous system" of the physical body; biochemical amino acids and peptides (neuropeptides), hormones, &tc.

NexGen Systemology : a modern tradition of applied religious philosophy and spiritual technology based on *Arcane Tablets* in combination with "*general systemology*" and "*games theory*" developed in the New Age underground by Joshua Free in 2011 as an advanced futurist extension of the "*Mardukite Chamberlains*"; also referred to as "*Mardukite Systemology,*" "*Metahuman Systemology*" and "*Spiritual Systemology.*"

objective : concerning the "external world" and attempts to observe Reality independent of personal "subjective" factors.

one-to-one : see "*A-for-A.*"

optimum : the most favorable or ideal conditions for the best result; the greatest degree of result under specific conditions.

orchestration : to arrange or compose the performance of a system.

oscillation-alternation : a particular type of (or fluctuation) between two relative states, conditions or degrees; a wave-action between two degrees, such as is described in the action of the *pendulum effect*; a flux or wave-like energy in motion, across space, calculable as time; in systematic processing, alternation is the shift between two direction flows on a circuit channel, such as *inflow* and *outflow*, or between two types of processing, such as *objective* and *subjective*; alternation of a POV creates "space."

pantheism : religious philosophies that observe God as inherent within all aspects of the Physical Universe.

paradigm : an all-encompassing *standard* by which to view the world and *communicate* Reality; a standard model of reality-systems used by the Mind to filter, organize and interpret experience of Reality.

parameters : a defined range of possible variables within a model, spectrum or continuum; the extent of communicable reach capable within a system or across a distance; the defined or imposed limitations placed on a system or the functions within a system; the extent to which a Life or "thing" can *be*, *do* or *know* along any channel within the confines of a specific system or spectrum of existence.

paramount : the most important; of utmost importance; "above all else."

participation : being part of the action; affecting the result.

patterns (probability patterns) : observation of cycles and tendencies to predict a causal relationship or determine the actual condition or flow of dynamic energy using a holistic systemology to understand Life, Reality and Existence as opposed to isolating or excluding perceived parts as being mutually separate from other perceived parts.

patron god : the most sacred deity of a region or city, of which most temples and religious services are directed; the personal deity of an individual.

PCL : see *"processing command line."*

perception : internalized processing of data received by the *senses*; to become *Aware of* via the senses.

personality (program) : the total composite picture an individual "identifies" themselves with; the accumulated sum of material and mental mass by which an individual experiences as their timeline; a "beta-personality" is mainly attached to the identity of a particular physical body and the total sum of its own genetic memory in combination with the data stores and pictures maintained by the Alpha Spirit; a "true personality" is the Alpha Spirit as Self completely defragmented of all erroneous limitations and barriers to consideration, belief, manifestation and intention.

perturbation : the deviation from a natural state, fixed motion, or orbit system caused by another external system; disturbing or disquieting the serenity of an existent state; inciting observable apparent action using indirect or outside actions or 'forces'; the introduction of a new element or facet that disturbs equilibrium of a standard system; the "butterfly effect"; in *NexGen Systemology*, *'perturbation'* is a necessary condition for the *ZU-line* to function as a *Standard Model* of actual *'monistic continuity'*—which is a *Lifeforce* singularity expressed along a spectrum with potential interactions at each degree from any source; the influence of a degree in one state by activities of another state that seem independent, but which are actually connected directly at some higher degree, even if not apparently observed.

phase (identification) : in *NexGen Systemology,* a pattern of personality or identity that is assumed as the POV from *Self*; personal identification with artificial "personality packages"; an individual assuming or tak-

ing characteristics of another individual (often unknowingly as a response-mechanisms); also *"phase
alignment."*

phase alignment or *"in phase"* : to be in synch or mutually synchronized, in step or aligned properly with
something else in order to increase the total strength
value; in *NexGen Systemology*, alignment or adjustment
of *Awareness* with a particular identity, space or time;
perfect *defragmentation* would mean being "in phase"
as *Self* fully conscious and Aware as an Alpha-Spirit *in*
present *space* and *time*, free of synthetic personalities.

philanthropy : charitable; the intention (or programmed
desire) to generously provide personal wealth and service to the well-being and continued existence of others.

physics : regarding data obtained by a material science
of observable motions, forces and bodies, including
their apparent interaction, in the Physical Universe (specific to this *beta-existence*).

physiology : a material science of observable biological
functions and mechanics of living organisms, including
codification and study of identifiable parts and apparent
systematic processes (specific to agreed upon makeup of
the *genetic vehicle* for this *beta-existence*).

pilfering : to steal in small quantities; petty theft.

pilot : a professional steersman responsible for healthy
functional operation of a ship toward a specific destination; in *NexGen Systemology*, an intensive trained
individual qualified to specially apply *Systemology Processing* to assist other *Seekers* on the *Pathway*.

ping : a short, high pitched ring, chime or noise that
alerts to the presence of something; in computer systems, a query sent on a network or line to another
terminal in order to determine if there is a connection to
it; in *NexGen Systemology*, the sudden somatic twinge
or pain or discomfort that is felt as a sensation in the
body when a particular terminal (lifeform, object,

concept) is 'brought to mind' or contacted on a personal communication channel-circuit; the accompanying sensations and mental images that are experienced as an automatic-response to the presence of some channel or terminal.

player (game theory) : an individual that is making decisions in a game and/or is affected by decisions others are making in the game, especially if those other-determined decisions now affect the possible choices.

point-of-view (POV) : a point to view from; an opinion or attitude as expressed from a specific identity-phase; a specific standpoint or vantage-point; a definitive manner of consideration specific to an individual phase or identity; a place or position affording a specific view or vantage; circumstances and programming of an individual that is conducive to a particular response, consideration or belief-set (paradigm); a position (consideration) or place (location) that provides a specific view or perspective (subjective) on experience (of the objective).

postulate : to put forward as truth; to suggest or assume an existence *to be*; to provide a basis of reasoning and belief; a basic theory accepted as fact; in *NexGen Systemology*, "Alpha-Thought"—the top-most decisions or considerations made by the Alpha-Spirit regarding the "*is-ness*" (what things "are") about energy-matter and space-time.

potentiality : the total "sum" (collective amount) of "latent" (dormant—present but not apparent) capable or possible realizations; used to describe a state or condition of what has not yet manifested, but which can be influenced and predicted based on observed patterns and, if referring to beta-existence, Cosmic Law.

POV : see "*point-of-view.*"

precedent : a matter which precedes or goes before another in importance.

precipitate : to actively hasten or quicken into existence.

preconception : to assign values or evaluate a reaction or response to a past "imprint" of something and treat it as present knowledge or experience.

prehistoric : any time before human history is properly recorded in writing; prior to c. 4000 B.C.

premise : a basis or statement of fact from which conclusions are drawn.

presence : the quality of some thing (energy/matter) being "present" in space-time; personal orientation of *Self* as an *Awareness* (*POV*) located in present space-time (environment) and communicating with extant energy-matter.

prevalent : of wide extent; an extensive or largely accepted aspect or current state.

probability : the causal likelihood for something to result, "effect" or manifest in and as a certain way, manner or degree, based on "observed evaluation" of programming and tendencies that follow Cosmic Law.

"process-out" or **"flatten a wave"** : to reduce *emotional encoding* of an *imprint* to zero; to dissolve a *waveform* or *thought-formed* "solid" such as a *"belief"*; to completely run a *process* to its end, thereby *flattening* any previously *"collapsed-waves"* or *fragmentation* that is obstructing the *clear channel* of *Self-Awareness*; also referred to as "processing-out"; to discharge all previously held emotionally encoded imprinting or erroneous programming and beliefs that otherwise fix the free flow (wave) to a particular pattern, solid or concrete *"is"* form.

processing, systematic : the inner-workings or "through-put" result of systems; in *NexGen Systemology*, a methodology of applied spiritual technology used toward personal Self-Actualization; methods of selective directed attention, communicated language and associative imagery that targets an increase in personal control of the human condition.

processing command line (PCL) or **command line** : a directed input; a specific command using highly selective language for *Systemology Processing*; a predetermined directive statement (cause) intended to focus concentrated attention (effect).

projecting awareness : sending out (motion) or radiating *"consciousness"* from *Self* ("I") to another POV.

proportional : having a direct relationship or mutual interaction with.

protest : a response-communication objecting an enforcement or a rejection of a prior communication; an effort to cancel, rewrite or destroy the existence or "isness" (what something "is") of a previous creation or communication; unwillingness to be the Point-of-View of effect or (receipt-point) for a communication.

Proto-Indo-European (PIE) : in Linguistic-Semantic Sciences, a hypothetical single-source Eurasian root language (c.4500 B.C.) demonstrating common origins of many "word-roots" found in European languages.

psychometric evaluation : the relative measurement of personal ability, mental (psychological/thought) faculties, and effective processing of information and external stimulus data; a scale used in "applied psychology" to evaluate and predict human behavior.

rationality / reasoning (game theory) : the extent to which a player seeks to play (make decisions, &tc.) in order to maximize the gains (or else survival) achievable within any given game conditions; the ability and willingness of an individual to reach toward conditions that promote the highest level of survival and existence and make the best choices and moves to see the desired goal manifest.

reactive control center (RCC) : the secondary (reactive) communication system of the *"Mind"*; a relay point of *Awareness* along the Identity's *ZU-line*, which is responsible for engaging basic motors, biochemical processes and any *programmed automated responses* of a living *beta* organism; the reactive Mind-Center of a living organism relaying communications of *Awareness* between causal experience of *Physical Systems* and the "*Master Control Center*"; it presumably stores all emotional encoded imprints as fragmentation of "chakra" frequencies of *ZU* (within the range of the "*psychological/emotive systems*" of a being), which it may *react* to as Reality at any time; in *NexGen Systemology*, this is plotted at (2.0) on the continuity model of the *ZU-line*.

reality : see "*agreement.*"

realization : the clear perception of an understanding; a consideration or understanding on what is "actual"; to make "real" or give "reality" to so as to grant a property of "beingness" or "being as it is"; the state or instance of coming to an *Awareness*; in *NexGen Systemology*, "gnosis" or true knowledge achieved during *systematic processing*; achievement of a new (or "higher") cognition, true knowledge or perception of Self; a consideration of reality or assignment of meaning.

receptacle : a device or mechanism designed to contain and store a specific type of aspect or thing; a container meant to receive something.

recursive : repeating by looping back onto itself to form continuity; *ex.* the "Infinity" symbol is recursive.

relative : an apparent point, state or condition treated as distinct from others.

relinquish : to give up control, command or possession of.

repetitively : to repeat "over and over" again; or else "repetition."

responsibility : the *ability* to *respond*; the extent of mobilizing *power* and *understanding* an individual maintains as *Awareness* to enact *change*; the proactive ability to *Self-direct* and make decisions independent of an outside authority.

resurface : to return to (or bring up to) the "surface" of that which has previously been submerged; in *NexGen Systemology*—relating specifically to processes where a *Seeker* recalls blocked energy stored covertly as emotional "*imprints*" (by the RCC) so that it may be effectively defragmented from the "*ZU-line*" (by the MCC).

Route-0 : a specific methodology from *SOP-2C* denoting "*Creativeness Processing*," as described in the text "*Imaginomicon*" (*Liber-3D*).

Route-0E : a specific methodology (expanding on *Route-0* from *Liber-3D*) denoting "*Conceptual Processing*" applied to *Ethics Beta-Defragmentation*, as described in the text "*Way of the Wizard*" (*Liber-Three* or *Liber-3E*).

Route-1 : a specific methodology from *SOP-2C* denoting "*Resurfacing Processing*," as described in the text "*Tablets of Destiny*" (*Liber-One*) as "RR-SP" (and reissued in "*The Systemology Handbook*").

Route-2 : a specific methodology from *SOP-2C* denoting "*Analytical-Recall Processing*," as described in the text "*Crystal Clear*" (*Liber-2B*) as "AR-SP" (and reissued in "*The Systemology Handbook*").

Route-3 : a specific methodology from *SOP-2C* denoting "*Communication-Circuit Processing*," as described in the text "*Metahuman Destinations*" (*Liber-Two*); also the basis for *SOP-2C* routine.

Route-3E : a specific methodology (expanding on *Route-3* from *SOP-2C*) denoting "*Ethics Processing*," as described in the text "*The Way of the Wizard*" (*Liber-Three* or *Liber-3E*); also related to "Standard Procedure R-3E."

scions : a descendant or offspring; an offshoot or branch.

Seeker : an individual on the *Pathway to Self-Honesty*; a practitioner of *Mardukite Systemology* or *NexGen Systemology Processing* that is working toward *Spiritual Ascension.*

Self-actualization : bringing the full potential of the Human spirit into Reality; expressing full capabilities and creativeness of the *Alpha-Spirit.*

Self-determinism : the freedom to act, clear of external control or influence; the personal control of Will to direct intention.

Self-evaluation : see *"psychometric evaluation."*

Self-honesty : the basic or original *alpha* state of *being* and *knowing*; clear and present total *Awareness* of-and-as *Self*, in its most basic and true proactive expression of itself as *Spirit* or *I-AM*—free of artificial attachments, perceptive filters and other emotionally-reactive or mentally-conditioned programming imposed on the human condition by the systematized physical world; the ability to experience existence without judgment.

self-sustained : self-supported; self-sufficient; independent.

semantics : the *meaning* carried in *language* as the *truth* of a "thing" represented, *A-for-A*; the *effect* of language on *thought* activity in the Mind and physical behavior; language as *symbols* used to represent a concept, "thing" or "solid."

semantic-set : the implied meaning behind any groupings of words or symbols used to define a specific paradigm.

sensation : an external stimulus received by internal sense organs (receptors/sensors); sense impressions.

sentient : a living organism with consciousness or intelligence; a "thinking" or "reasoning" being that perceives information from the "senses."

simulacrum : an tangible likeness, image, facsimile or

superficial representation that is similar to or resembles someone or something else; in *NexGen Systemology*, any *genetic vehicle* or physical body is considered a re-flective "simulacrum" of, and used as a "vessel-shell" by, the *Alpha-Spirit* or *Self* (I-AM), which otherwise maintains no true finite locatable form in *beta-existence*.

sine-wave : the *frequency* and amplitude of a quantified (calculable) *vibration* represented on a graph (graphic-ally) as smooth repetitive *oscillation* of a *waveform*; a *waveform* graphed for demonstration—otherwise rep-resented in *NexGen Systemology* logic equations as 'W*f*,' or in mathematics as the *'function of x'* (*fx*); graphically representing arcs (*parameters*) of a circular *continuity* on a *continuum*; in the *Standard Model of NexGen Sys-temology*, the actual 'wave vibration' graphically displayed on an otherwise static *ZU-line* (of Infinity) is a *'sine-wave'*.

singularity : in general use, "to be singular," but our working definition suggests the opposite of individuality (contrary to most dictionaries); in upper-level sciences, a "zero-point" where a particular property or attribute is mathematically treated as "infinite" (such as the "black-hole" phenomenon), or else where apparently dissimilar qualities of all existing aspects (or individuals) share a "singular" expression, nature or quality; additionally, in *NexGen Systemology*, a hypothetical zero-point when apparent values of all parts in a Universe are equal to all other parts before it collapses; in *Transhumanism*, a hy-pothetical "runaway reaction" in technology, when it becomes self-aware, self-propagating, self-upgradable and self-sustainable, and replaces human effort of ad-vancement or even makes continued human existence impossible; also, technological efforts to maintain an ar-tificial immortality of the Human Condition on a digital mainframe.

slate : a hard thin flat surface material used for writing on; a chalk-board, which is a large version of the origin-al wood-framed writing slate, named for the rock-type it was made from.

somatic : specifically pertaining to the physical body, its sensations and response actions or behaviors as separate from a "Mind-System"; also *"pings."*

SOP-2C : *Standard Operating Procedure #2C or Systemology Operating Procedure #2C*; a standardized procedural formula introduced in materials for *"Metahuman Destinations"* (*Liber-Two*); a regimen or outline for standard delivery of systematic processing used by *Systemology Pilots* and *Mardukite Ministers*; a procedure outline of systematic processing, which includes applications of *"Route-1," "Route-2," "Route-3"* and *"Route-0"* as taught for *Grade-IV Professional Piloting*.

space : a viewpoint or *Point-of-View* (POV) extended from any point out toward a dimension or dimensions; the consideration of a point or spot as an *anchor* or *corner* in addition to others, which collectively define parameters of a dimensional plane; the field of energy/matter mass created as a result of communication and control in action and measured as time (wavelength), such as "distance" between points (or peaks on a wave).

spectrum : a broad range or array as a continuous series or sequence; defined parts along a singular continuum; in physics, a gradient arrangement of visible colored bands diffracted in order of their respective wavelengths, such as when passing *White Light* through a *prism*.

standard issue : equally dispensed to all without consideration.

standard model : a fundamental *structure* or symbolic construct used to evaluate a complete *set* in *continuity* relative to itself and variable to all other *dynamic systems* as graphed or calculated by *logic*.

Standard Model, The (systemology) : in *NexGen Sys-*

temology—our existential and cosmological *standard model* or cabbalistic model; a *"monistic continuity model"* demonstrating *total system* interconnectivity "above" and "below" observation of any apparent *parameters*; the original presentation of the *ZU-line*, represented as a singular vertical (y-axis) waveform in space across dimensional levels or Universes (*Spheres of Existence*) without charting any specific movement across a dimensional time-graph x-axis; The Standard Model of Systemology represents the basic workable synthesis of common denominators in models explored throughout Grade-I and Grade-II material.

static : characterized by a fixed or stationary condition; having no apparent change, movement or fluctuation.

stoicism : pertaining to the school of "stoic" philosophy, distinguished by calm mental attitudes, freedom from desire/passion and essentially any emotional fluctuation.

sub-zones : at ranges "below" which we are representing or which is readily observable for current purposes.

successively : what comes after; forward into the future.

succumb : to give way, or give in to, a relatively stronger superior force.

Sumerian : ancient civilization of *Sumer*, founded in Mesopotamia c. 5000 B.C.

superfluous : excessive; unnecessary; needless.

superstition : knowledge accepted without good reason.

surefooted : proceeding surely; not likely to stumble or fall.

symbiotic : pertaining to the closeness, proximity and affinity between two beings that are in mutual communication or maintaining mutually validating interactions.

sympathy : a sensation, feeling or emotion—of anger, fear, sorrow and/or pity—that is a *personal reaction* to the misfortune and failure of another being.

system : from the Greek, "to set together"; to set or ar range things or data together so as to form an orderly understanding of a "whole"; also a *'method'* or *'methodology'* as an orderly standard of use or application of such data arranged together.

systematization : to arrange into systems; to systematize or make systematic.

Systemology : see *"NexGen Systemology."*

systems theory : see *"general systematology"*

Tablets of Destiny : the first professional publication of Mardukite Systemology, released publicly in October 2019; the first professional text in Grade-III Mardukite Systemology, released as *"Liber-One"* and reissued in the Grade-III Master Edition *"Systemology Handbook"*; contains fundamental theory of the *"Standard Model"* and *"Route-1"* systematic processing methodology.

terminal (node) : a point, end or mass on a line; a point or connection for closing an electric circuit, such as a post on a battery terminating at each end of its own systematic function; any end point or 'termination' on a line; a point of connectivity with other points; in systems, any point which may be treated as a contact point of interaction; anything that may be distinguished as an 'is' and is therefore a 'termination point' of a system or along a flow-line which may interact with other related systems it shares a line with; a point of interaction with other points.

thought-experiment : from the German, *Gedankenexperiment*; logical *considerations* or mental models used to concisely visualize consequences (cause-effect sequences) within the context of an imaginary or hypothetical scenario; using faculties of the Mind's Eye to *Imagine* things accurately with *considerations* that *have not* already been consciously experienced in *beta-existence*.

thought-form : apparent *manifestation* or existential *realization* of *Thought-waves* as "solids" even when only apparent in Reality-agreements of the Observer; the treatment of *Thought-waves* as permanent *imprints* obscuring *Self-Honest Clarity* of *Awareness* when reinforced by emotional experience as actualized "thought-formed solids" ("*beliefs*") in the Mind; energetic patterns that "surround" the individual.

thought-habit : reoccurring modes of thought or repeated "self-talk"; essentially "self-hypnosis" resulting in a certain state.

thought-wave or **wave-form** : a proactive *Self-directed action* or reactive-response *action* of *consciousness*; the *process* of *thinking* as demonstrated in *wave-form*; the *activity* of *Awareness* within the range of *thought vibrations/frequencies* on the existential *Life-continuum* or *ZU-line*.

threshold : a doorway, gate or entrance point; the degree to which something is to produce an effect within a certain state or condition; the point in which a condition changes from one to the next.

thwarted : to successfully oppose or prevent a purpose from actualizing.

tier : a series of rows or levels, one stacked immediately before or atop another.

time : observation of cycles in action; motion of a particle, energy or wave across space; intervals of action related to other intervals of action as observed in Awareness; a measurable wave-length or frequency in comparison to a static state; the consideration of variations in space.

timeline : plotting out history in a linear (line) model to indicate instances (experiences) or demonstrate changes in state (space) as measured over time; a singular conception of continuation of observed time as marked by event-intervals and changes in energy and matter across space.

tipping point : a definitive "point" when a series of

small changes (to a system) are significant enough to be *realized* or *cause* a larger, more significant change; the critical "point" (in a system) beyond which a significant change takes place or is observed; the "point" at which changes that cross a specific "threshold" reach a noticeably new state or development.

transhumanism : a social science and applied philosophy concerning the next evolved state of the *"Human Condition,"*; progress in two potential directions, either "spiritual" technologies advancing *Self* as an "Alpha-Spirit," or the direction of "external"-"physical" technologies that modify or eliminate characteristics of the *Body*; a theme describing contemporary application of material sciences emphasizing only "physical" and "genetic" parts of the *Human* experience, such as brain activity, cell-life extension and space travel; *NexGen Systemology* recently began distinguishing its emphasis on "spiritual technology" as *"metahumanism."*

transmit : to send forth data along some line of communication; to move a point across a distance.

traumatic encoding : information received when the sensory faculties of an organism are "shocked" into learning it as an "emotionally" encoded *Imprint*; a duplicated facsimile-copy or *Mental Image* of severe misfortune, violent threats, pain and coercion, which is then categorized, stored and reactively retrieved based exclusively on its emotional *facets*.

turbulence : a quality or state of distortion or disturbance that creates irregularity of a flow or pattern; the quality or state of aberration on a line (such as ragged edges) or the emotional "turbulent feelings" attached to a particular flow or terminal node; a violent, haphazard or disharmonious commotion (such as in the ebb of gusts and lulls of wind action).

unconscious : a state when *Awareness* as *Self* is removed totally from the equation of *Life* experience, though it continues to be recorded in lower-level re sponse mechanisms (fixed to a simulacrum or genetic vehicle) for later retrieval.

undefiled : to remain intact, untouched or unchanged; to be left in an original "virgin" state.

understanding : a clear 'A-for-A' duplication of a communication as 'knowledge', which may be comprehended and retained with its significance assigned in relation to other 'knowledge' treated as a 'significant understanding'; the "grade" or "level" that a knowledge base is collected and the manner in which the data is organized and evaluated.

validation : reinforcement of agreements or considerations as "real."

vantage : a point, place or position that offers an ideal viewpoint (POV).

Venn diagram : a diagram for symbolic logic using circles to represent sets and their systematic relationship; popularized by logician *John Venn*.

verbatim : precisely reproduced or duplicated communication *one-to-one* or "word"-for-"word" (*'A-for-A'*).

via : literally, "by way of"; from the Latin, meaning "way."

vibration : effects of motion or wave-frequency as applied to any system.

viewpoint : see *"point-of-view" (POV).*

vizier : a high ranking official; a minister-of-state.

wave-form : see *"sine-wave."*

wave-function collapse : see *"collapsing a wave."*

Western Civilization : modern contemporary culture, ideals, values and technology, particularly of Europe and North America as distinguished by growing urbanization, industrialization, and inspired by a history of rebellion to strong religious and political indoctrination.

will *or* **WILL** (5.0) : in *NexGen Systemology* (from the

Standard Model), the Alpha-ability at "5.0" of a Spiritual Being (*Alpha Spirit*) at "7.0" to apply *intention* as "Cause" from consideration or Alpha-Thought at "6.0" that is superior to "beta-thoughts" that only manifest as reactive "effects" below "4.0" and *interior* to the *Human Condition*.

willingness : the state of conscious Self-determined ability and interest (directed attention) to *Be, Do* or *Have*; a Self-determined consideration to reach, face up to (*confront*) or manage some "mass" or energy; the extent to which an individual considers themselves able to participate, act or communicate along some line, to put attention or intention on the line, or to produce (create) an effect.

ziggurat : religious temples of ancient Mesopotamia; stepped-pyramids and towers used for spiritual and religious purposes by Sumerians and Babylonians, many of which are presented as seven tiers, levels or terraces representing "Seven Gates" (or "7 Veils") of existence, separating material continuity of the Earth Plane from "Infinity" ("8").

ZU : the ancient Sumerian cuneiform sign for the archaic verb—*"to know," "knowingness"* or *"awareness"*; in *Mardukite Zuism and Systemology*, the active energy/matter of the "Spiritual Universe" (AN) experienced as a *Lifeforce* or *consciousness* that imbues living forms extant in the "Physical Universe" (KI); *"Spiritual Life Energy"*; energy demonstrated by the WILL of an actualized *Alpha-Spirit* in the "Spiritual Universe" (AN), which impinges its *Awareness* into the Physical Universe (KI), animating/controlling *Life* for its experience of *beta-existence* along an individual Alpha-Spirit's personal *Identity-continuum*, called a *ZU-line*.

Zu-**Line** : a theoretical construct in *Mardukite Zuism and Systemology* demonstrating *Spiritual Life Energy* (*ZU*) as a personal individual "continuum" of Awareness interacting with all Spheres of Existence on the Standard Model of Systemology; a spectrum of potential variations and interactions of a monistic continuum or singular *Spiritual Life Energy (ZU)* demonstrated on the Standard Model; an energetic channel of potential POV and "locations" of Beingness, demonstrated in early Systemology materials as an individual Alpha-Spirit's personal *Identity-continuum*, potentially connecting *Awareness (ZU)* of *Self* with "*Infinity*" simultaneous with all points considered in existence; a symbolic demonstration of the "*Life-line*" on which *Awareness (ZU)* extends from the direction of the "Spiritual Universe" (AN) in its true original *alpha state* through an entire possible range of activity resulting in its *beta state* and control of a *genetic-entity* occupying the *Physical Universe (KI)*.

Zu-Vision : the true and basic (*Alpha*) Point-of-View (perspective, POV) maintained by *Self* as *Alpha-Spirit* outside boundaries or considerations of the *Human Condition* "Mind-Systems" and *exterior* to beta-existence reality agreements with the Physical Universe; a POV of Self *as* "a unit of Spiritual Awareness" that exists independent of a "body" and entrapment in a *Human Condition*; "spirit vision" in its truest sense.

WOULD
YOU
LIKE
TO
KNOW
MORE
? ? ?

SYSTEMOLOGY
The Pathway to Self-Honesty

A Basic Introduction to
Mardukite Systemology

THE WAY INTO
THE FUTURE

A Handbook for
the New Human

a collection of
writings by
Joshua Free
selected by
James Thomas

Here are the basic answers to what has held Humanity back from achieving its ultimate goals and unlocking the true power of the Spirit and highest state of Knowing and Being.

"*The Way Into The Future*" illuminates the *Pathway* leading to Planet Earth's true "metahuman" destiny. With *excerpts* from "*Tablets of Destiny*," "*Crystal Clear*," "*Systemology—The Original Thesis*" and "*The Power of Zu*." You can help shine clear light on anyone's pathway!

Carefully selected by Mardukite Publications Officer, James Thomas, this critical *collection of eighteen articles, lecture transcripts and reference chapters* by Joshua Free is sure to be not only a treasured part of your personal library, but also the perfect introduction for all friends, family and loved ones.

(*Basic Grade-III Introductory Pocket Anthology*)

SYSTEMOLOGY
The Pathway to Self-Honesty

THE TABLETS
OF DESTINY
REVELATION

How Long-Lost Anunnaki Wisdom Can Change the Fate of Humanity

by Joshua Free

Mardukite Systemology Liber-One

second edition

Discover the origins of the Pathway to Self-Honesty with the book that started it all!

In this newly revised "Revelations" Academy Edition: Rediscover the original system of perfecting the Human Condition on a Pathway that leads to Infinity. Here is a way!—a map to chart spiritual potential and redefine the future of what is means to be human.

A landmark public debut for Grade-III Systemology and the foundation stone for reaching higher and taking back control of your DESTINY!

The revelation of 6,000 year old secrets, providing the tools and wisdom to unlock human potential...

SYSTEMOLOGY
The Pathway to Self-Honesty

CRYSTAL CLEAR
Handbook for Seekers

*Achieving
Self-Actualization
& Spiritual Ascension
in This Lifetime*

by Joshua Free

*Mardukite Systemology
Liber-2B*

second edition

Take control of your destiny and chart the first steps
toward your own spiritual evolution.

Realize new potentials of the Human Condition with
a Self-guiding handbook for Self-Processing
toward Self-Actualization in Self-Honesty using actual
techniques and training provided for the coveted
"Mardukite Self-Defragmentation Course Program"
—once only available directly and privately from the
underground International Systemology Society.

Discover the amazing power behind the
applied spiritual technology
used for counseling and advisement in
the Mardukite Zuism tradition.

SYSTEMOLOGY
The Pathway to Self-Honesty

METAHUMAN DESTINATIONS

The Original 2020 Professional Piloting Academy Course for Grade IV

by Joshua Free

Mardukite Systemology Liber-Two (2C,2D,3C) Revised 2-Volume Set

available individually

Drawing from the Arcane Tablets and nearly a year of additional research, experimentation and workshops since the introduction of applied spiritual technology and systematic processing methods, Joshua Free provides the ground-breaking manual for those seeking to correct—or "defragment"—the conditions that have trapped viewpoints of the Spirit into programming and encoding of the Human Condition.

Experience the revolutionary professional course in advanced spiritual technology for Mardukite Systemologists to "Pilot" the way to higher ideals that can free us from the Human Condition and return ultimate command and control of creation to the Spirit.

SYSTEMOLOGY
The Gateways to Infinity

IMAGINOMICON

Accessing the Gateway to Higher Universes
A New Grimoire for the Human Spirit

by Joshua Free

Mardukite Systemology
Grade-IV Metahumanism,
Wizard Level-0, Liber-3D

revised edition

The Way Out. Hidden for 6,000 Years.
But now we've found the Key.
A grimore to summon and invoke, command and control,
the most powerful spirit to ever exist.
Your Self.

Access beyond physical existence.
Fly free across all Gateways.
Go back to where it all began and reclaim that
personal universe which the *Spirit* once called *"Home."*

Break free from the Matrix;
control the Mind and command the Body
from outside those systems
— because *You* were never "human" —
fully realize what it means to be a *spiritual being*,
then rise up through the Gateways to Higher Universes
and *BE.*

SYSTEMOLOGY
The Gateway to Infinite Self-Honesty

THE WAY OF
THE WIZARD

Utilitarian Systemology

A New Metahuman Ethic

by Joshua Free

Mardukite Systemology Liber-3E

Grade-IV to Grade-V transition bridge

Your ticket off of a Prison Planet...
...and a Pathway leading to Spiritual Ascension!

Accumulated involvement in dangerous situations, states of confusion, unjust destruction and being at the effect end of faulty—or—blatantly false information, all lend to fragmented purposes that may very well be painted to appear "for our own good." Instead they are non-survival or counter-survival oriented, leading us away from routes to achieve "greater heights"—higher, more ideal, states of knowingness and beingness—including the Magic Universe immediately preceding this one.

Here then is a bridge from Grade-IV to Grade-V, the next great frontier of the *Pathway* crossed by participants in the "Freedom From" workshops led by Joshua Free in 2021.

SYSTEMOLOGY
The Gateways to Infinity

SYSTEMOLOGY-180
The Fast-Track to Ascension

A Handbook for Pilots

by Joshua Free

*Mardukite Grade-V
Systemology
Liber-180*

*Expert application of
all Grade-III and Grade-IV
training and techniques*

A perfected "metahuman" state for the Human Condition awaits; free of emotional turbulence, societal programming and an ability to be truly Self-Determined from the clear perspective of the actual Self, the Eternal Spirit or "I-AM" Awareness that is back of and beyond this existence—an "Angel" or "god" that has fallen only by its own considerations, by being convinced that it resides locally here on earth within a perishable human shell.

"Systemology-180" presents newly revised instruction from the Mardukite Academy to deliver the fastest results in climbing the Ladder of Ascension. Hundreds of exercises and techniques that progressively free you from bonds of the Human Condition and increase your spiritual horsepower enough to break the chains and attachments to the material world and an existence confined to a material body.

SYSTEMOLOGY
The Gateways to Infinity

SYSTEMOLOGY:

BACKTRACK

**Reclaiming
Spiritual Power &
Past-Life Memory**

by Joshua Free

*Mardukite Grade-V
Systemology
Liber-4*

*Transcripts of the
original lectures
with diagrams
and glossary*

We are all Spiritual Beings that have known a very long existence. Even before the evolution of Humans or Earth, we existed as other forms, in other times and spaces. We have descended down a very long *track* of potential Beingness and considerations, a *track* that parallels the allegory of "Fallen Angels" enticed by mundane bodies; only to be trapped in them and longing to *Ascend* again.

What if we could recover the long forgotten Knowingness of our past existences? What if we could reclaim our true Spiritual power that we have lost sight of? What if we could actually Backtrack our descent and return to the Source?

"*Backtrack*" documents the first advanced course given by Joshua Free to the Systemology Society for Grade-V. He candidly introduces the new Wizard-Level subject of Alpha-Defragmentation to Grade-III and Grade-IV alumni ready to embark on their next phase of the *Pathway*.

IN A WORLD FULL OF "TENS" BE AN
ELEVEN

THE METAPHYSICS OF STRANGER THINGS

TELEKINESIS,
TELEPATHY
SYSTEMOLOGY

by Joshua Free

Mardukite
Systemology
Liber-011

Experimental
exploratory
edition

Discover the metaphysical truth about the Universe—and maybe even yourself—as we explore what lies beneath the epic saga, *Stranger Things*. You're invited to a world where fantasy, science fiction and horror unite, and games like *Dungeons and Dragons* become reality.

Uncover a world of secret "mind control" projects, just like those at *Hawkins National Laboratory*. Decades of psychedelic experiments among other developmental programs for psychic powers, remote viewing, telekinesis (psychokinesis, PK) and more are revealed. Get an inside look at the operations of a real-life underground organization pursuing the truth about rehabilitating spiritual abilities for an actual "metahuman" evolution on planet Earth.

Premiere edition available in paperback and hardcover!

Commemorating the Mardukite 15th Anniversary!

NECRONOMICON
THE COMPLETE ANUNNAKI BIBLE
(Deluxe Edition Hardcover Anthology)
collected works by Joshua Free

The ultimate masterpiece of Mesopotamian magic, spirituality and history, providing a complete collection—a grand symphony—of the most ancient writings on the planet. The oldest Sumerian and Babylonian records reveal detailed accounts of cosmic history in the Universe and on Earth, the development of human civilization and descriptions of world order. All of this information has been used, since ancient times, to maintain spiritual and physical control of humanity and its systems. It has proved to be the predecessor and foundation of all global scripture-based religious and mystical traditions thereafter. These are the raw materials, unearthed from the underground, which have shaped humanity's beliefs, traditions and existence for thousands of years—right from the heart of the Ancient Near East: Sumer, Babylon and even Egypt...

Also available abridged in hardcover as:
"Necronomicon: The Compact Anunnaki Bible"

The Original Classic Underground Bestseller Returns!
10th Anniversary Hardcover Collector's Edition.

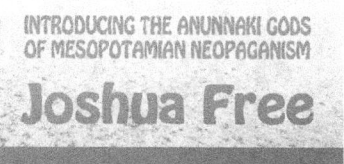

SUMERIAN RELIGION
Introducing the Anunnaki Gods
of Mesopotamian Neopaganism

Mardukite Research Volume Liber-50

by Joshua Free

Develop a personal relationship with Anunnaki Gods
—the divine pantheon that launched a thousand
cultures and traditions throughout the world!

Even if you think you already know all about the Sumerian Anunnaki or Star-Gates of Babylon... ＊ Here you will find a beautifully crafted journey that is unlike anything Humans have had the opportunity to experience for thousands of years... ＊ Here you will find a truly remarkable tome demonstrating a fresh new approach to modern Mesopotamian Neopaganism and spirituality... ＊ Here is a Master Key to the ancient mystic arts: true knowledge concerning the powers and entities that these arts are dedicated to... ＊ A working relationship with these powers directly... ＊ And the wisdom to exist "alongside" the gods, so as to ever remain in the "favor" of Cosmic Law.

Also available in paperback as *"Anunnaki Gods"* by Joshua Free.

"Babylonian Myth & Magic" (*Liber-51+E*) sequel now available!

∞

PUBLISHED BY THE **JOSHUA FREE** IMPRINT REPRESENTING

**The Founding Church of Mardukite Zuism
& Mardukite Academy of Systemology**

mardukite.com